Rúḥíyyih Khánum

Hussein Ahdieh
Hillary Chapman

Rúḥíyyih Khánum

Text Copyright © Hussein Ahdieh and Hillary Chapman
Publication Copyright © National Spiritual Assembly of the Bahá'ís of Australia Inc.
All Rights Reserved

ISBN 978-1-925320-52-7 (softcover)
ISBN 978-1-925320-53-4 (hardcover)
ISBN 978-1-925320-55-8 (ePub)
First edition, 2023

Distributed by
Bahá'í Distribution Services
173 Mona Vale Rd, Ingleside, NSW, 2101

bds@bahai.org.au
www.bahaibooks.com.au

Body text typeset in 12/19pt Minion 3
Other text typeset in Montserrat
Front-cover text Scala Pro

Cover design by René Steiner @ Steiner Graphics, Toronto

Bahá'í
Publications
Australia

This book is dedicated

to youth all over the world

who strive to serve humanity

Foreword

This remarkable book is dedicated to youth all over the world. However, since it gives an inspiring and intimate look at the life of Rúhíyyih Khánum quoting from her personal diaries and those of Violette Nakhjavani, her closest companion, it deserves the attention of all who are interested in the Bahá'í Faith.

Rúhíyyih was born Mary Maxwell into the distinguished Bahá'í family in Canada, the Maxwells. Her mother was devoted to 'Abdu'l-Bahá, the son of Bahá'u'lláh, the Prophet-Founder of the Bahá'í Faith, and was privileged to have Him stay in her home. His love and teachings surrounded Mary at an early age.

Her father, William Maxwell, an artist and distinguished architect became a Bahá'í after meeting 'Abdu'l-Bahá.

Little Mary was a very precocious child and quite outspoken. At a very early age, she instructed her mother who was about to punish her for being late for dinner and said 'Don't punish me for the small things.' At age nine, when 'Abdu'l-Bahá sent the Tablets of the Divine Plan to American, she was one of the two children asked to unveil the Tablets.

Mary was a free spirit and loved animals. On one of several trips to the Holy Land to visit 'Abdu'l-Bahá with her mother, she took one cat, one rat, two dogs, one hen and one snake. Both parents encouraged Mary in her creativity and her love for the arts. At Green Acre Bahá'í School, she wrote four plays and performed in a Shakespearean play.

Although she had been in the Holy Land many times, at age fifteen she made her first personal pilgrimage along with several Canadian friends. Shoghi Effendi, who was the Head of the Faith at that time, asked her to see him. He spent time advising her on her education encouraging her to study economics, literature, and Persian. He later gave her lessons in Persian, often teasing her about her pronunciation of Persian words.

Inspired by her mother, Mary actively taught the Bahá'í Faith, especially in Germany. She wrote regular reports to Shoghi Effendi about her activities as a pioneer as was the custom. He encouraged her to contribute to the development of the Bahá'í Administrative Order by helping to form Local Spiritual Assemblies. Shoghi Effendi wrote to her: 'I am delighted with your accomplishments. My heart is filled with hope and gratitude.'

In 1937, when Mary was chosen as the bride of Shoghi Effendi, he gave her the title 'Amatu'l-Bahá Rúhíyyih Khánum' meaning 'Handmaiden of Glory' Rúhíyyih Khánum. He wanted their marriage to be seen by Bahá'ís as a union of East and West, linking their destinies. He gave her a precious gift on the day of the wedding. After the wedding, Rúhíyyih Khánum became his constant companion and helpmate assisting him with his massive correspondence and with the Covenant-breakers (those who didn't accept him as Guardian, some from his own family). She said that the Guardian was like a man whose 'skin had burned off ... even time could not remove the scars of it.'

Rúhíyyih played a critical role in the construction of the Shrine of the Báb, representing Shoghi Effendi in negotiating prices with engineers, contractors, and importers.

In 1951, Shoghi Effendi created the first International Bahá'í Council, the forerunner of the Universal House of Justice. He appointed Rúhíyyih Khánum to that Council and named her as a Hand of the Cause (responsible for the expansion and coordination of the Cause around the world).

When Shoghi Effendi died, Rúhíyyih Khánum was one of the nine Hands of the Cause chosen to live in the Holy Land to coordinate the affairs of the Bahá'í World to win the goals on the Ten-Year Crusade. She was later the Chief Teller at the election of the first Universal House of Justice and introduced it at the First Bahá'í World Congress in London in 1963.

In talking to the Guardian one day, she said to him 'what will happen when you are no longer with us?' The Guardian replied: 'I suppose you will go and visit the friends in different countries and encourage them.'

Mass teaching had been one of the main themes of the Bahá'í World Congress. In the 1950s, large numbers of people became Bahá'ís in India and Africa. Rúhíyyih Khánum decided to go first to India first and then Africa with her constant companion Violette Nakhjavani, daughter of Hand of the Cause, Musa Banani. They travelled thousands of miles by plane, Jeep, boat and foot visiting over 100,000 new Bahá'ís in cities, villages and at the new Teaching Institutes. She had a beautiful voice and constantly emphasised that there are two doors through which people can recognise truth: the door of the mind or intellect and the door of the heart or intuition.

When they went to Africa, they bought a Land Rover because many roads were impassable due to the rains. Rúhíyyih Khánum drove this vehicle over 30,000 miles to more than 30 countries, and she even learned how to repair it herself.

Their last major trip was to Latin America. They were particularly interested in reaching Indigenous peoples and were received everywhere with great respect. They travelled by small boat up the rivers of the Amazon region. She called this trip the 'Green Light Expedition' and the story of their expedition along the Amazon and Orinoco Rivers is well documented in a documentary by that name. Rúhíyyih Khánum hoped that by filming this, Bahá'ís would be inspired to respond to 'Abdu'l-Bahá's call to travel among Indigenous people.

In all her travels, her eloquent tongue lifted the hearts and visions of all who heard her. She was, indeed, as the Guardian described her, 'Amatu'l-Bahá — Handmaiden of Glory'.

Judge Dorothy Nelson, 2022 C.E. / 179 B.E.

Introduction

From Thomas Ahdieh Grant, Bahá'í youth:

A big part of anyone's life on earth is to meet the challenges of the day. The Universal House of Justice tells us that 'every generation of young believers' is given an opportunity 'to make a contribution to the fortunes of humanity, unique to their time of life.'[1] Do you think about what your contribution may be at this moment in human history?

One way to get ideas about our contribution is to pray and study the Holy Writings. Another is to look at the needs of those around us and make efforts to better the world. Yet another is to be in the field of service with friends with whom we can collaborate. Another is to learn about other young people in human history who did all of this and see if we can learn from their experiences.

The life of Rúhíyyih Khánum is one such life. At every stage, she was alive to the needs of the day and lifted herself up to meet them.

When we think about Rúhíyyih Khánum, many of the images that come to mind are from the middle and later part of her life after she married the Guardian of the Faith and became a part of the Holy Family, later when she was named a Hand of the Cause of God, and as she travelled the world and visited over 100 countries.

This incredible woman, though, was once a child and a youth just like you and me. She had dreams and hopes. She loved animals, was very enthusiastic about learning, and had lots of energy. She also loved 'Abdu'l-Bahá and alongside her mother and father, she was devoted to the teachings of Bahá'u'lláh and arranged her life in such a way that she would promote its teachings and principles.

When Rúhíyyih Khánum was born her name was Mary Maxwell. She was born in Montreal, Canada, and her parents were May Maxwell and Sutherland Maxwell. Both of her parents were dynamic and brilliant people, and their marriage was devoted to service. Mary Maxwell had the great honour of meeting 'Abdu'l-Bahá when she was two years old. She first met Him in New York and then again in Montreal when He stayed at their home. What an honour and life-altering experience to meet the Perfect Exemplar at such a tender age.

Mary was introduced early on to the vision of the Faith, and she became devoted to it. Notwithstanding her mother's extensive time away from home, Mary thrived. She was actively engaged in Bahá'í activities at every stage of her life. She was present at the gathering where the Tablets of the Divine Plan were first introduced to a group of American believers and as a youth was the one to unveil them.

Although this book is a full biography of Rúhíyyih Khánum's life, the episodes from her childhood and youth will be especially of interest to readers who are themselves young people figuring out the course of their lives. It is also interesting to see how the capacity built during these young years of Mary's life—capacities to accompany others, to learn, to have courage, to stay committed to the Centre of the Faith—were ones that served her well in her decades of service to the Cause until her very last breath.

This book was written especially with youth in mind. It will be uplifting and educational for you and help you respond to the call for selfless service in this great Day of God.

From the authors:

Our goals for this book are to have the reader:

1. Follow Rúhíyyih Khánum on her travels all over the world. Understand how early Bahá'í communities came into existence.

2. See how she overcame challenges, remained steadfast in her Faith in Bahá'u'lláh despite all the tests, and served the Bahá'í community at crucial moments in its history.

3. Understand the role of 'Abdu'l-Bahá, Shoghi Effendi, and the Universal House of Justice; learn more about the Bahá'í teachings.

4. Appreciate the high station of Shoghi Effendi and the Universal House of Justice.

5. Gain familiarity with world geography, cultures, and languages from around the world.

Dr Hussein Ahdieh, Hillary Ioas Chapman

Authors' notes about sources

The information in this book is drawn almost entirely from primary sources except for one major secondary one:

The Maxwells of Montreal: Volumes 1 and 2. This exhaustively researched, two-volume history of the Maxwell family is written by her dear friend travelling companion, Violette Nakhjavani, who spent more time with Rúhíyyih Khánum than almost anyone else. The authors have extensively mined the personal correspondence of Rúhíyyih Khánum, her mother, May Bolles, and her father, Sutherland Maxwell, from these volumes. This is the only current source on the life of Rúhíyyih Khánum's immediate family.

The Priceless Pearl. The definitive biography and witness to the life of Shoghi Effendi from the uniquely intimate perspective of his wife, Rúhíyyih Khánum. She was his companion, secretary, and 'shield' during many challenging times. This invaluable first-hand witness to the greatness of his station and accomplishments as well as the severe tests he had to endure, captures the intensity of the life of this great figure, and gives the reader a feeling for him as a person.

Amatu'l-Bahá Rúḥíyyih Khánum visits India. Rúhíyyih Khánum made several major trips to India to support the mass-teaching efforts that were underway, especially those in rural areas. This book is a first-hand account written by Violette Nakhjavani who was with her during all these trips.

The Great Safari of Hand of the Cause Rúḥíyyih Khánum. Rúḥíyyih Khánum and Violette Nakhjavani undertook a series of teaching trips throughout Africa. A serialised account written by Mrs Nakhjavani appeared in editions of the Bahá'í News from 1970 to 1973 so that the generality of Bahá'ís could follow their trip and learn from the visits to the many mostly rural Bahá'í communities.

The information for Part I (chapters 1-4) is from *The Maxwells of Montreal: Volumes 1 and 2.*

The information for chapters 5, 6, 7, 8, 9 and 10 is from *The Priceless Pearl.*

The information for chapters 14, 15, and 16 is from *Amatu'l-Bahá Rúḥíyyih Khánum visits India.*

The information for chapters 17, 18, and 19 is from *The Great Safari of Hand of the Cause Rúḥíyyih Khánum.*

All other sections of the book are either general knowledge or from sources specified in the endnotes.

All words attributed to 'Abdu'l-Bahá or Shoghi Effendi that are not from their published writings or talks should be regarded as pilgrims' notes, that is, as the recollection of the hearer and not as their exact words, nor authoritative.

Opening

One day 'Abdu'l-Bahá was resting in the home in Montreal, Canada, of May and William Maxwell, and He recalled:

> ... I was resting on the chaise longue* in my bedroom and the door opened. The little girl came in to me and pushed my eyelids up with her small finger and said, 'Wake up, 'Abdu'l-Bahá!'[2]

This little girl, the subject of our story, was Mary Maxwell, later called Rúhíyyih Khánum.

Mary Maxwell was the daughter of May and William Maxwell, two devoted Bahá'ís who lived in Montreal, Canada. May became an active and gifted teacher of the Bahá'í Faith, and William an accomplished architect and sincere Bahá'í. Little did they know how extraordinary a life their daughter would have: Bahá'í teacher, wife of Shoghi Effendi, and world traveller as a Hand of the Cause of God.

Because Mary Maxwell was so close to both of her parents growing up, we start our story with her amazing mother, May Maxwell.

---

*   A lounge with a backrest at one end.

Part 1

The early years before marriage

Chapter 1

Mary was very close to her mother, May Maxwell. May was not only her mother in the sense that she was the one who gave birth to her, fed her, clothed her, and loved her, she was also the 'mother of her soul.' She fed Mary the knowledge that God loved her and that His Love surrounded her, and that Bahá'u'lláh was His Manifestation who had brought new teachings for this New Day.

May's life was guided by 'Abdu'l-Bahá the way a flower that faces the sun soaks in its rays and grows day by day. She was constantly writing to 'Abdu'l-Bahá about her many Bahá'í activities, and He responded to her with loving words of advice, encouragement, and wisdom.

May had a very generous heart. She welcomed people of every background into her home and always wanted to create harmony and understanding. She never held grudges nor was she mean to any person. May also showed this great kindness towards those closest to her. It's often easier to be loving to strangers than to people in one's own family with whom we must live with every day but she never allowed anyone in the family to go to bed angry or hurt. When her husband Sutherland went to work she always kissed him goodbye and on occasion told her stubborn little daughter: 'Mary, go and kiss your father, it's most unkind of you not to, he needs your love.'[3]

The Maxwell home was a home of harmony filled with the spirit of May's love. Mary later remembered that since her childhood, she had 'never found its like anywhere.'[4]

May Maxwell was a spiritual person even as a child.

One day when she was fifteen, she was walking through the English countryside, the sun was out, and the sounds of birds filled the air. Then a deep spiritual feeling came into her heart. She saw that the sky above, the meadow below, and all the sounds of the creatures were a part of her and were filled with great spiritual meaning. She realised that the secret of the universe was that God was present everywhere and surrounded her and would be with her always.

She dreamt one night that she was being carried up into the sky. When she looked down, she saw the earth wrapped in chains and waxen seals like those used to close letters in those days. Suddenly these all started to crack and break open, and she saw a word written across the earth. When she woke up, she could only remember two of the letters of that word: B and H.

May was a dreamer—a creative, imaginative person—and a seeker—she wanted to know about the deeper meanings of life. She was not interested in the ordinary, unimportant things of this life.

But she had also been born in 1870 into a well-to-do family in the leafy town of Englewood, New Jersey, and society had rules and expectations for a young woman: find a suitable husband and start a family.

A marriage was not about having romantic feelings for someone or being in love, though that would always make it more enjoyable. In those days, a young woman like May did not date. Young men would have to ask for permission to visit her in her parents' house.

Upper class young women were introduced at formal balls as available for marriage. A wealthy friend of May's mother, Phoebe Hearst, decided to introduce May at the balls in Washington DC. She even had gowns specially made for May to wear in the morning, afternoon, and evening. Despite these efforts and many admirers, May did not marry.

May was attractive, educated, and refined, but she seemed to her family to belong to another world. She did not like shallow conversations and relationships. She had deep thoughts and great sincerity. She spent lengthy periods feeling ill or depressed and staying in bed and then other times she was lively and sociable. Her family began to be alarmed. She was extremely sensitive to everything happening around her. This pattern of illness continued for the rest of her life.

May's mother decided to move the family to Paris in 1894 because her son Randolph was going to study at the arts school, the Ecole des Beaux Arts. She hoped that being in a new city would improve May's poor health.

Phoebe Hearst let them stay in the guest rooms of her luxurious apartment in Paris. May lay in bed like an invalid. Much to her dismay, guests who came in the evenings talked only about the eligible bachelors in Paris much to her dismay. Yet she clung to hope that God was always near and that 'surely the Light will come.'[5]

And so it did. In Paris, she found her spiritual destiny.

A large and diverse group was travelling with Phoebe Hearst. Americans in Paris wondered where such a group was going. It included a Lebanese doctor, Ibrahim Kheiralla, and Hearst's butler, Robert Turner,* as well as an American couple, Mr and Mrs Getsinger. People speculated that they were going on an exciting trip down the Nile or to the Greek islands. But there were people who were suspicious about the strange religion that Kheiralla and the Getsingers belonged to and were concerned that Mrs Hearst was becoming involved with it.

But Phoebe Hearst did not tell anyone the true reason for this voyage. She wanted to avoid any gossip or unwanted attention—her son was a very famous and controversial newspaper owner, William Randolph Hearst.

They were going to visit 'Abdu'l-Bahá and the Sacred Tomb of Bahá'u'lláh in Palestine. This was the first pilgrimage group ever to go from the West to the Holy Land.

After arriving in Paris, Phoebe Hearst was shocked when she walked into the dark bedroom and saw the condition of May Maxwell whom she had introduced at the debutante balls in Washington DC.

---

* The first Black American Bahá'í.

May had dark circles under her eyes, and her body was deeply sunk into the pillows of her bed. Mrs Hearst and other friends agreed that this was more than a medical problem.

Phoebe Hearst and the group were determined to rouse her. Edward Getsinger suggested that his wife Lua,* a spiritually wise and insightful woman, might be best able to help her.

Lua entered May's room and sat next to her. She told her about the true nature of the trip. For the first time, May heard the name of 'Abdu'l-Bahá and learned of the teachings of the Bahá'í Faith. The words she most remembers from Lua were:

'There is a Prisoner in 'Akká who holds the key to peace.'[6]

When May heard these words, she sat up in bed, exclaimed 'I believe, I believe' and straight-away fainted from being overwhelmed.

This was the turning point in May's life. In Paris, 1898, her 'whole being came alive with the love of her Lord and service to Him.'[7]

The Hearst group gathered at 13 Quai D'orsay on the Seine River in Paris to leave for Egypt. Though there was great excitement among the group, they had to be careful and used code such as 'headquarters' to describe where they were going. To get to Haifa and 'Akká, they had to first travel to Egypt. From there they'd go in small groups to visit 'Abdu'l-Bahá. As foreigners from the West they would stand out,

---

* Lua Getsinger was training to be an actress in Chicago when she learned of the Bahá'í Faith from attending Dr Kheiralla's classes.

and they did not want to bring unwanted attention to 'Abdu'l-Bahá who was still a prisoner of those who opposed the Faith.

May arrived in the Bay of Haifa on 16 February 1898. In Paris, Phoebe Hearst bought special gowns for May to wear for her meeting with 'Abdu'l-Bahá as well as jewels to give as gifts to the women of His family. But when it came time to meet 'Abdu'l-Bahá the next morning, she had to rush and did not have time to put on the fancy clothes. When she was ushered into the room, she saw the Master among a group of people.

'Abdu'l-Bahá was the living embodiment of love. May remembered that the pilgrims '... learned the mystery of Divine Love'[8] from the Master. He had no interest in the things of this world. When He was presented with all the jewels brought by Mrs Hearst for the family, He turned to them and said: '... all these I accept because they come from your love but 'Abdu'l-Bahá has no need of material gifts. He wants your hearts for God alone, purified from all else save God.'[9] Later the pilgrims learned that the jewels were sold in the market, and the proceeds given to the poor.

'Abdu'l-Bahá's parting words to May on that first pilgrimage would set a pattern for the rest of her life:

And now I give you a commandment which shall be for a Covenant between you and Me—that ye have faith, that your faith be steadfast as a rock that no storms can move, that nothing can disturb, and that it endure through all things even to the end; even should ye hear that your Lord has been crucified, be not shaken in your faith; for I am with you always, whether living or dead, I am with you to the end. As ye have faith so shall your powers and blessings be. This is the balance-this is the balance-this is the balance.

... look at Me, follow Me, be as I am ... ye must die to yourselves and to the world, so shall ye be born again and enter the Kingdom of Heaven. Behold a candle how it gives its light. It weeps its life away drop by drop in order to give forth its flame of light.[10]

May and Mary Maxwell, circa late 1910.

May and Mary Maxwell, circa late 1910.

Mary Maxwell, circa 1914.

May and Mary Maxwell in Alexandria, Egypt, 1923.

Mary Maxwell, circa 1926.

Mary Maxwell, circa 1926.

Mary Maxwell, summer 1934.

William Sutherland Maxwell.

Chapter 2

William Sutherland Maxwell was born in 1874, in Montreal, Canada, into a family of Scottish background which moved to Canada in the 1820s. His family raised him to believe in the 'Importance of family, diligent work, and integrity.' [11] Even as a young person, William was self-motivated. He believed in working hard and striving for excellence.

William was not rigid in his thinking. He was quite inventive and enjoyed searching for solutions to technical problems.

After high school, William decided to go directly into his chosen profession, architecture. He wanted to learn the profession by doing it rather than just by studying it. He picked up the fundamentals by working as an apprentice draughtsman in his brother's firm.

Next, William took a job at a workshop of the Society of Architects in Boston. He always attended free lectures to learn more about his craft and joined the Boston Architectural Club to keep up with the latest developments. He was a person who could teach himself and learn on his own. For example, he kept sketchbooks in which he drew features of buildings that he found interesting as well as scenes of villages and people.

William believed very much in *doing things*—practice—to learn rather than by studying theories in school. It didn't mean that school didn't have any value—it did—but being an artist meant you had a spiritual gift and should strive day and night to bring it out and show you deserve that gift.

He was a talented artist. He developed a vast knowledge of architecture and design and was able to see the world from many different perspectives. He came up with fresh and highly original ideas. His wife later wrote that he had the 'charm of originality.'[12]

William was truthful, courteous, and friendly towards all people—and he was upright, meaning he always dealt with people honestly. At the firm in Boston, his great talent quickly became obvious.

His hand could draw any image he had in his mind. Soon he wanted to see more. He applied to one of the famous workshops in Paris which had trained many American architects, and with his brother's financial help, he moved to Paris to study.

Among Sutherland's friends in Paris was Randolph, May's brother. He invited the Canadian over to their home in Paris. May's mother was eager to meet Sutherland as a potential husband for her daughter.

But May reacted differently. At the end of the evening she said to her brother, 'Don't ever bring that big Canadian here again!' She complained to her brother that Sutherland stared at her the whole time. The truth was that Sutherland was smitten with May that very evening, and she didn't know it.

But May was in love with the Bahá'í Faith. Teaching the Faith was the central purpose of her life. Her teaching efforts resulted in a small but growing and vibrant Bahá'í community in Paris. From that community many others were born.

First, there was Brenetta Herrman, an American painter, who recognised the truth of the Faith immediately.

Then, there was Theodora Mackay, a well-known singer in Paris, who poured out her heart to May after hearing the teachings of the Faith on unity and became a confirmed Bahá'í.

Laura Barney was attracted to the teachings through May while in Paris. Barney later went on to compile a series of talks by 'Abdu'l-Bahá, *Some Answered Questions*, which became a major source of guidance for Bahá'ís. She married Hippolyte Dreyfus, the first French person to become a Bahá'í, and her mother became a believer as well.

Juliet Thompson, an American painter, was also a friend of May's and became a passionate follower of 'Abdu'l-Bahá. She spent much time with Him in New York City, and wrote a diary about her experiences which we can still read today.

May was also the spiritual teacher of Marion Jack, a Canadian who got to know May's family through the art students at Ecole des Beaux Arts. She went on to become one of the most courageous of Bahá'í pioneers, moving to Bulgaria where she endured years of poverty and other difficulties caused by World War II.

Mason Remey was another of May's spiritual children. He came from a distinguished American family and was refined and charming as a person but he had become restless. Remembering him in Paris, May wrote that she 'never met a more thirsty soul.'[13] He became one of the most knowledgeable of the early American Bahá'ís and served the Faith for decades, eventually being appointed a Hand of the Cause.

Another seeker who became a Bahá'í during those years in Paris and who went on to serve with great distinction was Agnes B. Alexander. She opened Japan to the Faith and was later appointed a Hand of the Cause.*

During the summer of 1901, the most extraordinary teaching experiences of May's life took place. Her family wanted her to come away with them on summer vacation. 'Abdu'l-Bahá asked her to stay in Paris a while longer. Her family was upset that May did not join them but soon 'Abdu'l-Bahá's wisdom was evident: Thomas Breakwell, a young Englishman whom she had met, came to her door one morning and told her that after meeting her he felt spiritually transformed. He now believed that Jesus had returned. May told him he had found the truth and proceeded to tell him all about the Faith. This young man became extraordinarily devoted and was much loved by 'Abdu'l-Bahá.

May's mother, though, was not interested in all this nearly as much as in getting her daughter married. But when it came to suitors, May was not interested in physical attention—she had plenty of that because she was pretty—what she wanted was a spiritual bond.

---

* Title given to individuals appointed by Shoghi Effendi who assisted him in the propagation and protection of the Bahá'í community and the teaching of the Faith around the world. Bahá'u'lláh and 'Abdu'l-Bahá appointed Hands of the Cause as well. Unfortunately, later in life, despite his many years of distinguished service to the Faith, Mason Remey did not remain faithful to the Covenant.

Sutherland Maxwell was coming over often with the excuse of helping her brother with his work deadlines. May could tell, though, that Sutherland was interested in her. She wondered to herself if he could be a seeker and see the truth of the Faith? This was the most important thing to her.

The letters between the two became friendlier and less formal, with Sutherland writing things like, 'What an unfinished affair my life would have been without your friendship ...' and 'Dear, each moment seemed a second, each second was a precious jewel, my sole regret was that Time is such a hasty creature.'[14]

In the Spring of 1900, May was asked to sit for a portrait. She didn't want to do this until she realised that it would give her an opportunity to talk with Sutherland while she was being painted. They were both so busy that there was no free time otherwise. May saw these meetings as an opportunity to teach Sutherland the Faith. Once she wrote to him: 'That is one reason why my heart longs to share the Truth with you, not alone because it is the dearest and highest & best to which man can attain, but because then I shall feel indissolubly united with you ...'[15]

May realized that though Sutherland was not a Bahá'í, he was spiritually-minded and a very good man, and that she could learn much spiritually from him as well. The two were engaged on 14 November 1900. In a tablet, 'Abdu'l-Bahá gave His consent for them to marry: 'Do all that is in thy power for the spirituality of the fiancé, that he may become celestial and divine. After thy marriage, spare no effort in this, that haply his heart may be illumined by the light of the Kingdom.'[16]

May and William were married on 8 May 1902, in the parish of Christ Church, Woburn Square, London. William's work was in Montreal so the young couple had to live in Canada, far away from the Paris that May had come to love. Paris was where she had come to believe in Bahá'u'lláh and where she had nurtured a whole Bahá'í community into existence. She found it very difficult to leave her 'spiritual children' for whom she felt so much responsibility.

May also continued to long for a spiritual union with her new husband. May fell into one of her deep illnesses, and she believed this time that the only cure was to open the spiritual eyes of her husband and make their marriage a spiritual one. Sutherland was interested in beauty, design, art, and architecture while May's thoughts were always on spiritual matters. For Sutherland, his love for May was what brought him close to God.

One of the approaches May took to teaching the Faith—whether she was aware of it or not—was to encourage those who were studying the Faith with her to teach it to others. She did the same with her husband:

There is no work in the world today that can compare with this—it is the highest service we can render to God & I realize how fitted you are for this—for people love you so—your own

beautiful, unselfish nature influences them deeply & they do
not forget this influence which is the light of the Spirit ... [17]

One day, though, Sutherland said to May: 'You are involved more
and more in your Bahá'í work and I in my professional work; we
are drifting apart.' May reminded him that she had explained before
their marriage how great her commitment was to the Faith, and this
was her priority so she stated: 'If I must, I will go alone on this chosen
path.' Sutherland thought a while and said, 'I will go with you all the
way.' [18]

Sutherland fully realised the place of the Faith in his wife's life.
But May also knew of friends who had devoted all their time to the
Faith whose marriages had fallen apart. She had come to see what
a rare gem of a man Sutherland was and did not want to lose him.
'Abdu'l-Bahá counselled her:

Deal with thy husband with consideration; be as kind to him
as possible, and advise him with all courtesy. He will come
under the outspread shadow of the Cause and will obtain
his light from the lamp of guidance. Give him a firm promise
that, if he should believe, he will find his greatest happiness in
both worlds.

This is a promise that shall not be belied. [19]

By 1904, Sutherland considered himself a Bahá'í. 'Abdu'l-Bahá wrote:
'It is a sign of great bounty that thine honourable husband has allied
himself with thee, and thou hast led him to the Threshold of God.' [20]

May affectionately wrote to Sutherland that, to him, she was now: 'Wife-sweetheart-friend-companion-and your spiritual mother! Just think of it!'[21]

The Maxwells built a house on Pine Avenue in Montreal. With May's loving and welcoming spirit and Sutherland's sense of beauty and design, the house became the place where the Montreal Bahá'í community was nurtured.

With the house finished, the young couple could fulfil another of May's dreams: a second pilgrimage to the Master so Sutherland could meet Him face to face.

One day when Sutherland was at the table with the Master, he said, 'The Christians worship God through Christ; my wife worships God through You; but I worship him direct.'

The Master smiled and asked him: 'Where is He?'

Sutherland replied: 'Why God is everywhere.'

The Master explained: 'Everywhere is nowhere.' He went on to say that when we worship on our own, we end up believing in our own ideas and following our own imaginary thoughts. God, the Unknowable One, made Himself known through His Manifestation Who in this day and age was Bahá'u'lláh. To know God meant to know Bahá'u'lláh. Sutherland listened carefully and accepted the Master's words. This is the moment he became a truly confirmed Bahá'í.

Another day on the pilgrimage May was speaking with 'Abdu'l-Bahá and talked to him about having children. When she explained that she thought she could not have children, the Master said that this was not true and promised her she would have one. She wept as she remembered 'His voice, the light of His glance, the mysterious all-enveloping potency of His Eternal Spirit!'[22]

On 8 August 1910, a baby girl, Mary, was born to May and Sutherland Maxwell.

'Abdu'l-Bahá wrote to them:

Thanks be to God! Thy greatest wish to have a child hath been granted, and what thou didst ask hath been realized, and thy friends and relatives may thus be led to certitude and assurance. I ask God that thou wilt be both the spiritual and physical mother of that luminous child, so that she may receive her portion of the bestowals of the Sun of Truth.[23]

And later:

Do thou kiss both cheeks of thy sweet daughter who hath just begun to talk.[24]

Chapter 3

'Abdu'l-Bahá was an exile and a prisoner for over forty years. All the major responsibilities of the family fell on Him because He was the eldest son. He had to provide for the numerous family members as well as the Bahá'í followers who were in exile with them. He had to deal with all the officials to secure any kind of comfort or security. There were constant plots against Him from those in 'Akká who wanted to destroy the Faith. He had to tend to anyone who became sick even when He fell ill Himself; He suffered from frostbite, dysentery, and tuberculosis among other illnesses, some of which recurred throughout His whole life. When there were several Bahá'ís who died, and there was no room anywhere else, He had to sleep in the room where the bodies were kept.

On top of all of this, He also went throughout 'Akká taking care of the poor, even giving His own clothes and bedding. He paid a doctor to help those who were sick. He never forgot even one person, no matter how unimportant they appeared to others. The courage and humility with which He faced years of terrible difficulties with not a moment's relief, won the respect and admiration of the people of 'Akká such that they referred to Him as the 'Master'. Bahá'u'lláh described His eldest son as '*... this sacred and glorious Being, this*

Branch of Holiness ...' and wrote *'... well is it with him that hath sought His shelter and abideth beneath His shadow.'*[25]

In 1908, 'Abdu'l-Bahá and the other Bahá'í exiles were freed; there had been a great political change in the Turkish government, and all political prisoners were set free. 'Abdu'l-Bahá had landed in 'Akká a young man of twenty-four and took His first steps of freedom as an older man of sixty-four years with many ailments and an aching body.

And yet because His suffering was in the path of His Beloved, Bahá'u'lláh, He had always been truly free. Freedom, He said, was not 'a matter of place. It is a condition.' Suffering in the path of God elevated one's soul. The greatest prison of all was the self and 'When one is released from the prison of self, that is indeed a release.'[26]

The first place He visited after He was no longer officially a prisoner was the tomb of His Father, Bahá'u'lláh, at Bahjí, where He planted a garden.

Then He set His sights on planting a much larger garden: He would travel to Europe and America and proclaim the Teachings of Bahá'u'lláh.

In 1910, 'Abdu'l-Bahá left Palestine for Egypt from where ships sailed for the West. His health was so weak that a prolonged illness delayed His departure for a year. In 1911, He made a five-month journey throughout Western Europe, guiding and encouraging the small Bahá'í groups and proclaiming the Faith in churches and other public places. During these journeys to the West, the Greatest Holy Leaf, 'Abdu'l-Bahá's sister, was responsible for the affairs of the Faith.

By 1912, the Master set off on His long and arduous journey to the United States despite His physical frailty. On 25 March, He and the men travelling with Him boarded the large steamer, the S.S. Cedric, bound for the West.

The United States and Canada were going to be blessed with the presence of 'Abdu'l-Bahá. Shoghi Effendi described the journey's significance:

'Abdu'l-Bahá's historic journeys to the West, and in particular His eight-month tour of the United States of America, may be said to have marked the culmination of His ministry, a ministry whose untold blessings and stupendous achievements only future generations can adequately estimate. As the day-star of Bahá'u'lláh's Revelation had shone forth in its meridian splendour at the hour of the proclamation of His Message to the rulers of the earth in the city of Adrianople, so did the Orb of His Covenant mount its zenith and shed its brightest rays when He Who was its appointed Center arose to blazon the glory and greatness of His Father's Faith among the peoples of the West. [27]

'Abdu'l-Bahá was the living embodiment of the Covenant—He was the 'Centre of the Covenant'. The Covenant was the agreement of Bahá'u'lláh with His followers that they would turn to 'Abdu'l-Bahá after His passing and look to Him as the infallible Interpreter of the Bahá'í Writings, their source of authority and guidance. This Covenant was written into Bahá'u'lláh's Will and Testament, the

Kitáb-i-'Ahd, the 'Book of the Covenant'. Because of the Covenant, the Bahá'í Faith did not split apart—many people tried to divide the Bahá'ís from 'Abdu'l-Bahá—and because the Faith has remained one religion without sects and divisions, it has the power to unify the world.

And so—like the rising sun—'Abdu'l-Bahá's life of service reached its noonday height on this trip through the West which Shoghi Effendi described as the 'greatest exploit ever to be associated with His ministry.'[28]

When 'Abdu'l-Bahá was in New York City, May was able to visit Him. When she came into His presence, Mary was not with her. The Master asked about Mary, and May answered that she was not well so she had not brought her. The Master looked surprised and wondered why she had not brought her sick child to Him. Of course, May returned immediately to get Mary. When He saw the little girl, 'Abdu'l-Bahá gazed at her lovingly and gave her an orange, telling her that this would heal her. May let her daughter hold the orange but not eat it. Many decades later when Mary passed away, the old orange was found among her things with a note telling this story.

Most thrilling of all for May was that 'Abdu'l-Bahá agreed to come to Montreal and stay in their home.

Sutherland Maxwell met 'Abdu'l-Bahá with two carriages at the Windsor train station in Montreal on 30 August 1912. At this time the Master was sixty-eight years of age. Sutherland was nervous about having 'Abdu'l-Bahá in their home. At the last minute, he wondered if the furniture in the guest bedroom was good enough, and he ran out to buy new furniture. Of course, this was wholly unnecessary. 'Abdu'l-Bahá did not care at all about fancy expensive things. He refused all personal gifts and gave them instead to others including the poor. When Bahá'ís wanted to buy Him a ticket on the fanciest ship in the world, the *Titanic*, He refused. He only cared about turning the hearts of people towards God and ensuring the Bahá'ís were united among themselves.

May remembered the Master's arrival in their home:

In the fullness and splendour of a summer moon 'Abdu'l-Bahá arrived on the night of August 30th. As he entered the home of Bahá'í friends on Pine Ave., many watched from their windows to catch a glimpse of the white-robed majestic figure whose advent had been so eloquently heralded thro' all the press. [29]

When 'Abdu'l-Bahá stepped into the Maxwell home He said, 'This is my home.' [30]

As May wrote, the neighbours were all watching because they had read about 'Abdu'l-Bahá in the newspaper. The Bahá'í community of Montreal had been very active in letting newspapers know about this important visit. Newspapers referred to Him as 'the venerable Apostle of Peace,' the 'Eastern Sage,' the 'Oriental Seer,' and 'the Persian Prophet' though He tried to convince journalists not to use the last title. [31] 'Abdu'l-Bahá, of course, wanted to be known as a 'servant' because servitude to others was the highest station to which any human being can attain.

The Master gave eight formal talks in churches and to organisations and groups as well as gatherings in the Maxwell home. People from all backgrounds came to see and hear the Master: Arabs, Turks, Americans, French Canadians, Jews, and Persians, as well as Canadians.

Several times 'Abdu'l-Bahá spoke about and used the word 'reality':

Reality is one; it does not admit plurality.[32]

This oneness, this 'reality', was at the basis of everything in the world. The Manifestations of God were all 'servants of reality'. The Manifestations all taught the same reality. So all religions were one. They all came from the same source.

The Revelation of Bahá'u'lláh contained within it the truths of all previous religions with the new teachings for a new day:

His [Bahá'u'lláh's] revelation of the Word embodies completely the teachings of all the Prophets, expressed in principles and precepts applicable to the needs and conditions of the modern world, amplified and adapted to present-day questions and critical human problems. That is to say, the words of Bahá'u'lláh are the essences of the words of the Prophets of the past.[33]

To understand this, a person had to 'investigate reality' for themselves. They had to leave aside their own opinions and those of their parents, teachers and others and learn about the Bahá'í Faith with an open mind free of any prejudices or attachments. On their own, they had to decide, whether or not the Claims of Bahá'u'lláh are true.

'Abdu'l-Bahá felt cold during the first night He spent in the Maxwell home. May lit a fire in the fireplace for Him. He looked around and asked for the child, Mary, but she was sleeping. He told them not to disturb her.

Having 'Abdu'l-Bahá in her home made May more joyful and excited than she had ever been. She longed to do nothing else but serve the Master. Even the small daily chores now had great significance, and she delighted in doing them. She had a glow about her.

Mary was two years old by then, full of life and spirit. May worried that sometimes her active little one was misbehaving. Her daughter later wrote:

One day the Master, in the drawing room, caught little Mary up in His arms and tried to kiss her; I say tried advisedly for He did not succeed as the small, strong, chubby and highly independent infant gave him such a slap on the face that the shock knocked the turban off His head! Then began a mad chase around the drawing-room in which the Master pursued the elusive and indignant child. Mother always said at that moment she could have gladly killed me. She managed to say, 'Oh, 'Abdu'l-Bahá, she is very naughty! What shall I do to punish her.' By this time the Master had succeeded in catching and kissing me. 'Leave her alone,' He said, 'she is the essence of sweetness.[34]

The power of attraction of the Master was so strong, and there was so much coverage in the papers about Him that the number of people coming to the Maxwell house grew every day. He decided to move to the Windsor Hotel which had much more room. The bad-tempered cook was so upset at His leaving the house that she begged May, 'Tell him I will work my fingers to the bone if He will stay!'

But there were many people to teach. 'Abdu'l-Bahá left for the Windsor Hotel and then on 9 September, He left Montreal, and on 3 December, He boarded the ship to leave America. The ripples He left behind would turn into a large and dynamic Bahá'í community and His collected talks from this trip, published as *The Promulgation of Universal Peace*, has served as a great source of guidance and inspiration for Bahá'ís all over the world.

When 'Abdu'l-Bahá arrived in England, He cabled May:

SAFELY ARRIVED LONDON. REMEMBERED ALWAYS. GREETINGS MAXWELL KISS BABY, ABBAS.[35]

Mary Maxwell turned four years old when World War I broke out. Most people thought this would be a quick war. It turned into one of the most devastating wars in history causing unimaginable suffering—around nine million soldiers and ten million civilians lost their lives. Almost all the kings and queens of Europe fell from power.

Despite the incredible suffering, the war led to an even worse conflict, World War II, the bloodiest war in human history.

May and Sutherland were busy building up a more peaceful world by teaching the Bahá'í Faith and assisting with raising money for the Bahá'í House of Worship that was going to be built in the United States. A Bahá'í House of Worship is a nine-sided temple where people of all faiths or no faith may come and pray and find spiritual relief.

The Maxwells were also busy with the joy of raising their little girl. May remembers Mary playing in a Canadian winter during those war years:

> *As soon as she could toddle on her fat sturdy legs she would go out to play and be swallowed up from view in those huge snow banks higher than the tallest man which often characterize the Canadian winters. She could stay out for hours in the coldest weather and would come in caked with snow, her fat cheeks like red apples, her blue eyes lit with joy and tell her mother quite seriously that she loved the snow better than anything in the world.*
>
> *Her little voice was sweet and clear, she always spoke very distinctly, and from her earliest childhood used the most remarkable language. When she was about three years old she remarked with a pleasant smile to a guest, 'I only live for these Canadian winters' and then added cheerfully, 'I am really very sorry for those children in New York and Boston who have to scrape around to find a little snow to slide on.* [36]

May and Sutherland noticed that their child was interested in everything and anything—especially animals. She wrote to Santa Claus asking for a pet monkey, a kitten, a puppy, a goldfish, a chicken, and a parrot. One day, she came running into the house to tell her mother that a big fat caterpillar was crossing the sidewalk. Then she added quickly so that her mother would not worry about the creature, that the caterpillar was not near enough to get stepped on. One summer evening, she came in from their garden very excited to be holding a large toad in her hands.

Her parents encouraged her to speak her mind. Because she was an only child, she got the full attention of her parents so she learned how to speak with adults and developed a big vocabulary. Even though she was very young, she showed that she could think logically. Once when her mother punished her for being late, she replied:

You must not punish me so much for such a small thing—I am only little and young and I don't know the hard things about life yet. You must only punish me a little bit for little things, and a lot when I am very bad.[37]

May wanted her active and intelligent little girl to have an education that would allow her to be more creative than a regular school would allow. So she changed the top floor of their family house into a kindergarten and hired a Montessori teacher. Montessori education was based on the ideas of Maria Montessori who thought that classes should be structured so that children could explore and follow their own interests. It was becoming popular at the time. Several other children from among May's extended family and friends joined, and a class of eight students was formed and went on through the war years.

The Maxwell family had money so they were able to hire a governess. May was frequently away from her daughter, often for extended periods of time. She travelled to visit family and to get away from the cold in Canada which affected her health.

May did not forget about her daughter when she was away. She constantly wrote her long letters in which she told her what she was doing and always gave her loving encouragement and spiritual advice.

Being in a privileged family, Mary also had servants who worked in her home. She had a German maid, Emma Replisch, who acted as her nanny. In early 1915, May was feeling very sick and so she moved with May and Emma to the seaside in New York. One day, Emma went out for a walk. But she did not return. The police came to the cottage in which they were staying to tell them that a body had washed up on the shore. The police asked May to come and identify the body. May was very ill and asked Mary to go for her. Mary was able to go and identify the body of their dear Emma. She remembers that she was not afraid at all. In some ways, Mary had a very sheltered life and, in other ways, she had to face the grown-up things of life early on. Her mother and she later spoke about death and its meaning. Mary told her mother she believed that when she died her heart would fly to 'Akká and be with 'Abdu'l-Bahá.

In the summer of 1916, World War I was raging. The Brusilov offensive in Russia resulted in more than 2,000,000 dead and injured human beings and in the Battle of the Somme more than 1,000,000 soldiers were killed or wounded. In the middle of these bloody and violent years, 'Abdu'l-Bahá wrote messages to the Bahá'ís in North America* on small postcards calling on them to arise and teach the Faith. These are the *Tablets of the Divine Plan*.

Shoghi Effendi tells us that the *Tablets of the Divine Plan* are part of the 'charter' of the new world order brought by Bahá'u'lláh.† A 'charter' is a written document that establishes and gives rights and a mission to a country or organization. In this case, it is the Bahá'í Administrative Order—the institutions at the Bahá'í World Centre, the Spiritual Assemblies, and the teaching of the Faith.

'Abdu'l-Bahá wrote that He had not seen much progress in the growth of the Bahá'í community: 'It is about twenty-three years that the fragrances of God have been diffused in America, but no adequate and befitting motion has been realised, and no great acclamation and acceleration has been witnessed.'‡

Those who arose to teach the Faith must have 'a pure heart,' 'a rejoiced spirit,' and 'an eloquent tongue,' so that 'the oneness of humanity may pitch her canopy in the apex of America and all the nations of the world may follow the divine policy.' This way America

---

*   Including the territory of Greenland.

†   There are three Writings that make up this charter according to Shoghi Effendi. The other two are Bahá'u'lláh's *Tablet of Carmel* and the *Will and Testament* of 'Abdu'l-Bahá.

‡   Tablet to the Southern States.

could come to lead the world spiritually as it already did materially. 'Abdu'l-Bahá told them that one of the Manifestations of God had promised that if a 'person become the cause of the illumination of one soul, it is better than a boundless treasury.'[38]

The Tablets of the Divine Plan challenged Bahá'ís to arise. May received the two Tablets for the Dominion of Canada on 19 August 1916. They hit her like a thunderbolt. She knew now that she would have to think beyond her community of Montreal, or those she knew in Boston and New York and travel more widely to spread the Faith. In the coming years, she travelled more for the Faith and her administrative responsibilities multiplied. Sutherland also became more involved in the administration of the Faith.

But this increase in their activity and May's absences happened just as their daughter was going into adolescence. May had to figure out how to balance her obligations to the Cause with meeting the needs of her child who was growing up fast. She explained this to her daughter:

Some day when you are married and know the sweetness and pain of motherhood, you will realize more fully that however often I have been compelled to leave you since you were a little child, for the sake of this great Cause in which we are united; and however lonely you may have often been, you never suffered alone, because I was always with you, I felt for you more deeply than you could ever realize, and it is out of the pangs of this mighty motherlove that my spiritual motherhood to you has been born.[39]

She wrote Mary letters constantly that were full of affection and news of teaching activities:

> *Mother feels very near to her little girl all the time—especially when I have the joy of telling people about ʻAbduʼl-Bahá …*

> *I hope my little girl is well and happy and I am <u>longing</u> to see you and hold you in my heart …*

> *I send my tender love to you & Isa & my heart is at rest because I know you both live every moment in the sunshine of His Great love …*

> *My darling little girl—What a big page to write on to a little girl? But you are so big now, and I am wondering why you do not write to Mother? Ask Daddy to hold your hand while you write me a little letter—because I love you so much my darling, and I long to have a letter from you.*[40]

Through all these letters, May kept up with her daughter's activities, told her about her teaching work, encouraged her in her own personal growth and development, and conveyed her love for her. Most importantly, she knew that by arising to teach the Faith in response to the Master's *Tablets of the Divine Plan*, she was setting an important example for Mary to follow.

Receiving the *Tablets of the Divine Plan* was a high point in the life of the Maxwells. The Tablets were formally unveiled in a ceremony in New York City. Mary was asked to participate in the ceremony—her first official act for the Bahá'í community; she would have many more! In April 1919, at the McAlpine Hotel in New York City, Mary, dressed in soft pink silk and another Bahá'í teenager from Montreal, Elizabeth Coristine, unveiled all the Tablets that the Master had written to them. This Divine Plan was the source of many Bahá'í teaching plans later initiated by Shoghi Effendi and the Universal House of Justice. The *Tablets of the Divine Plan* were like a trumpet blast, and they set the worldwide expansion of the Faith in motion.

Chapter 4

Shoghi Effendi was studying at the University of Oxford in 1921. He wanted to master the English language so that he could return to the Holy Land and serve his grandfather as a secretary and translator. He longed for nothing more than to be by his Grandfather's side helping with the increasing work of the growing Bahá'í community.

On 28 November, he got a call from Major Tudor Pole, the secretary of the British Bahá'í group from whose office all correspondence for Bahá'ís was distributed. He had to come to Pole's office in London to pick up a message.

When Shoghi Effendi arrived in the office, he found no one there. On the table, though, he saw a telegram with 'Abdu'l-Bahá's name on it. It read: 'His Holiness 'Abdu'l-Bahá ascended Abhá Kingdom. Inform friends. Greatest Holy Leaf.'[41]

Shoghi Effendi collapsed.

When this news reached Canada, the Bahá'ís there were shocked. May Maxwell took to her bed. She almost lost the will to keep living.

To Bahá'ís, 'Abdu'l-Bahá *was* the Bahá'í Faith in human form, the Centre of the Covenant who held the Bahá'í community together. He was the one to whom all could turn as the perfect example of how to be a Bahá'í and to whom they could constantly turn to for guidance.

Now He was gone from this world. The great love of the Bahá'ís for the Master now turned to grief and uncertainty about the future.

But 'Abdu'l-Bahá had not left them alone. He had written a *Will and Testament* in which He described His grandson, Shoghi Effendi, as 'the blest and sacred bough' whose shade 'shadoweth all mankind,' and stated that he was 'the Sign of God, the chosen branch, the Guardian of the Cause of God.'

The Covenant was not broken and had not ended. Shoghi Effendi was now the head of the Faith towards whom all Bahá'ís could turn in relation to all matters large and small, in whose hands all its administrative affairs now rested, and whose interpretations of the Bahá'í Writings were authoritative. The unity of the Bahá'í community was secure.

This news was a great comfort to the Maxwells but May remained in deep shock. Sutherland suggested she go to the Holy Land to meet Shoghi Effendi.

The trip to Haifa took a long time because of May's poor health. Mary had to take care of her mother even at a young age. Her mother really depended on her and the personal assistant who travelled with them. Though only twelve years old, Mary had to organise the travel arrangements as they went, which was a great responsibility for one so young.

Mother and daughter stayed in the pilgrim house across the street from 'Abdu'l-Bahá's home. May needed a lot of rest because she had made a long trip by boat during which she suffered from insomnia.

One morning there was a visitor at the door. Mary, who was tending to her mother, went to answer it. When she opened it a young man stepped into the house. Mary stood up tall. She was worried about her mother's health and didn't want her to be disturbed. She said, 'Mrs. Maxwell is resting; who is it who wants to see her?'

The young man answered, 'I'm Shoghi Effendi.'

Mary was so shocked and embarrassed that she ran back into her mother's room and hid in the pillows. Her mother asked her what was wrong, and Mary could only answer, 'He's here, he's here.' Once she understood what her daughter meant, May told her to pull herself together and to go tell the Guardian that she would be out soon to greet him.

During the next weeks, Shoghi Effendi became a spiritual doctor to May. He diagnosed the source of her depression—she was grieving 'Abdu'l-Bahá's loss deeply and letting herself be taken away by dark thoughts. Once he told her, 'Mrs. Maxwell, the thoughts you are thinking are not true!'[42]

He knew that she needed to become physically active, regain her strength, and serve the Cause in order to get rid of the psychological depression. He also knew that she ruminated on death.

May took notes of Shoghi Effendi's advice and the passages from the Writings he quoted:

There is naught in the Universe but God.

Concept of annihilation ... has been conducive to <u>dispersion</u> <u>weakening</u> of human thought.

Man must believe in <u>truth</u> not in <u>error</u>—because the plane of thought leads to the plane of spirit in reality so that he may <u>advance</u> <u>upward</u> and <u>higher</u> to spiritual <u>perception</u> of the continuity of the human reality.

Faith is <u>conscious</u> knowledge.[43]

These talks with Shoghi Effendi helped May understand her condition and improve but she still had a way to go. Sometimes getting out of psychological depression can take many steps, but the Guardian had given her all the knowledge she needed to do so.

In those early years, Shoghi Effendi went to Switzerland during the summer. This time, before he left, he recommended that May convalesce in Egypt. Once May, Mary, and their attendant reached the resort in Egypt, May sank back into dark thoughts, especially about death. She missed 'Abdu'l-Bahá whom she had seen the last time she was in Egypt. But she also received news from her husband that his beloved brother was terminally ill. Both parents also looked to Mary for help with communication and for support. She had to be unusually mature and responsible at an early age.

Mary, even with such responsibilities and sensitive to all the distress of both of her parents, remained a free spirit who loved animals. She travelled, for example, with a whole group of animals which she collected along the way. She wrote to her father about their trip: 'We will take the zoo and baggages: 1 cat 1 rat 2 dogs 1 hen, we ate the other one.'[44] May was patient with her daughter about this but it was difficult to be in the hotel room at night with birds, a snake, a cat and 'a white rat with red eyes.' When the time came to return to the Holy Land, May gave her daughter instructions for preparing for the trip that included the animals: 'Please get rid of your birds, pack the rat carefully at the last moment. Have you got your snake?'[45]

Back in the Holy Land, Mary wrote to her father in a letter showing that her heavy responsibilities were always with her: 'I think Mother is improving very much. She walks a little every day and one day when Shoghi Effendi came here and went to the Tomb we all went with Him and Mother walked about 200 yards without any help. She was a little tired the next day and got right over it.'[46]

In this second part of their long-extended pilgrimage, Shoghi Effendi spent a great deal of time with May to change the way she was feeling. To do that he changed her thinking. He filled her mind with inspiring ideas of the future and helped her to see the vision of Bahá'u'lláh's unfolding World Order. He explained that these new and young Bahá'í institutions had a spiritual basis and that she had a significant role in helping others understand the development of this Administrative Order which was a new stage for the Bahá'í world. She could play a vital role by educating the friends about this.

Shoghi Effendi's guidance gave May a new sense of mission. She returned to the West feeling that she had a purpose and threw herself into the middle of Bahá'í activities. She wrote letters constantly to others to help guide them in their Bahá'í work which had a significant effect on the development of Bahá'í communities. Most importantly, she now felt a deep sense of devotion to Shoghi Effendi.

~

Growing up, Mary spent long periods of her time without her mother. Nevertheless, her mother wrote letters to her constantly that were full of spiritual and emotional guidance and encouragement. She always stressed the development of spiritual qualities and service:

> *I hope you have not forgotten your promise to take dear old Mrs. Pomeroy out at least twice a week. You have so much to give and share with others, and this is the greatest happiness in life, and poor, old Mrs. Pomeroy is old and sick and very poor, and I know how she would appreciate these drives, especially if you sometimes go with her yourself ...* [47]

Here May praises her daughter's spiritual qualities:

> *This is just to tell you, my darling, how much I love you, and appreciate your beautiful qualities. I know you went back to New York for my sake, so that I could be alone and rest ... this is the sign of your growth and development, your deeper spiritual understanding of life and its true purpose. Also, you are much more selfless in little things such as doing without things you want, helping me to economize (not my strong point), and in regulating your window at night to suit your guests rather than yourself.* [48]

Mary, at fourteen, had great responsibilities on her shoulders for the maintenance of their household, including hiring and firing people. She wrote to her mother:

> ... I have not had a minute to write before now. In the first place the cook affair is in an awful mess because that perfect JEM [sic] of a scotch cook you engaged didn't turn up, she said you told her that the chauffeur would wait on the table. Of course I informed her very gently that she was entirely mistaken and that we would talk it over after dinner; as Mr. de Trembly was coming to dinner I was in a hurry but still showed her where everything was and was nice to her ... After dinner I went down stairs and gave her clean linen and talked to her about the house and said I thought she would get on all right and that if there was anything at all she wanted I would be very glad to show her where it was ... After the meeting was over some one phoned up and said that her sister did not like the place and was spending the night with her and would call for her things in the morning!!!!![49]

Her mother's response showed how much she valued and respected her daughter and how closely the two consulted together:

> I must congratulate you on your good management of the household and with regard to the cook. You are a very capable girl and I am sure that by the time I get back home, I shall find a far better housekeeper than myself.[50]

In her mother's absence, Mary also acted as hostess to the guests who came to the house. In those days, visits to a person's home were much more formal than today. Guests sat down and had tea or a meal, and the places at the table had to be set. Mary got a lot of practice in how to organise a formal meal, how to make her guests feel welcome, and how to guide conversation. The main purpose of many of these gatherings was to make friends for the Faith. Mary loved to do this with her mother who was her role model:

I feel dear the importance of these contacts at this time cannot be over-estimated and I cannot believe that so many doors are opening to me unless I am meant to seize the opportunities they afford. I can barely wait for you to come home and help me. There is only one way to do these things and that is through continuous social contact. [51]

Both parents encouraged their daughter in her creativity and her love of the arts. The one year she spent in a regular school, she performed in a Shakespearean play. She wrote many poems, for which she won a prize at school. Her mother encouraged her to write her own stories. At Green Acre, Mary wrote four plays and performed in several others. Her father encouraged her to pursue her interest in sculpture: 'You have a real talent for sculpture, stick to it ...' [52]

To help her form her own Bahá'í identity, May wanted Mary to go on a pilgrimage without her parents when she reached fifteen, the age of maturity. In April, 1926, Mary and two friends boarded a boat in New York and set out for the Holy Land.

Her mother wrote her encouragingly about the pilgrimage:

*'Abdu'l-Bahá said that the pilgrims coming to the shore of the
'City of the Tideless sea' coming to his Presence brought with
them the cup of their heart and filled it to overflowing from
that vast ocean of truth, and then he added, 'My only sorrow
is that the cups they bring are so small.'*

*Now you, May, have a larger cup, a fuller and greater capacity
than I ever had and I feel that you are going to bring back to
us all and to Canada and to all the youth movement, such a
power of Divine love, sweetness, wisdom and understanding
which shall profoundly affect us all ...* [53]

When Mary went to pray at the tomb of 'Abdu'l-Bahá, she had a
powerful experience. While she was praying, she felt that her mother
was praying with her as well. She cried and then, gradually, through
prayer, her tears became feelings of joy and happiness. This is how she
wanted to greet Shoghi Effendi—with joy and gladness, not tears—to
help uplift his spirits.

Shoghi Effendi had many difficult issues to work on that often
distressed him so he did not pay much attention at first to the young
pilgrim from Canada. While praying, Mary criticised herself because
she felt she must have done something wrong. Then, much to her
great joy and relief, Shoghi Effendi asked for her to come see him.
He spent time advising her on her education, encouraging her to
study economics, sociology, literature, as well as learn the Persian

language. Shoghi Effendi also assured her that one day her father would vie with her mother in service to the Cause in Haifa.[54] May was overjoyed at this advice from the Guardian. He later wrote to her mother: 'My earnest hope is that Mary may follow in your footsteps and render memorable services to the Cause you love so well.'[55]

May wrote to Sutherland of the profound change that had come over their daughter since her pilgrimage:

> *Everyone speaks of the extraordinary change in Mary since her trip to Haifa and the progress she has made and we must do everything in our power to cherish this exquisite flower of spirituality that is just blooming in her heart which is best done by showing her the utmost love at all times for that is the only all-conquering power.*[56]

After this pilgrimage, Mary as well as her mother were now wholly devoted to Shoghi Effendi and assisting him in the progress of the Cause. The Maxwells moved as a united threesome. So, soon, the father would be following in their footsteps.

In early 1933, May and Mary went together to teach the Bahá'í Faith in the city of Washington DC.

These were the days of the Jim Crow laws when buildings, trains, public rest-rooms, hotels, and many other public spaces were segregated by race. Signs were placed above water fountains and doors telling people whether a white person or a Black person* was allowed to use it. The DC Bahá'í community struggled to have meetings that included both races. Such gatherings were highly unusual in society. White people who wanted to learn more about the Faith, and who thus came to a meeting and saw Black people, might object or turn away from the Faith. There were white Bahá'ís who believed that teaching meetings should be only for whites or only for Blacks, so that race would not create a barrier for people learning more about the Faith. Other Bahá'ís thought that their meetings must reflect the Bahá'í teachings and not imitate society, even if it made certain white people uncomfortable.

May and Mary had study classes on the Faith on Tuesday nights focused on the issue of race unity. Mary often thought about this subject to the point where she wrote a 600-page novel, *Green Amber*, with that as its main theme. At these classes, the two races mixed freely.

When May left Washington DC, Mary stayed on and continued the integrated classes. She was criticised by a few older Bahá'ís for being too radical, but her mother encouraged her to maintain the standard set by 'Abdu'l-Bahá, so Mary persisted. The Bahá'í Assembly finally gave her formal permission to hold inter-racial meetings. These continued and were held in different locations including the

---

* The term 'Negro' was used in those days. Today the term is no longer considered appropriate and 'African-American' or 'Black American' is commonly used.

home of a Black believer. Mary's enthusiasm and purity of heart broke through to people and won them over.

Her mother wrote about Mary's efforts to Shoghi Effendi:

In Washington Mary became launched as a young and independent teacher of the Cause! For altho we worked together—held meetings—spoke to both colored and white groups—and at Howard University—side by side—yet Mary carried on an intensive teaching campaign among the cultured Negro population ... [57]

In 1935, Mary brought all that energy for teaching to Germany where she was travelling to meet her family. She fell in love with the beauty of the country:

The Rhine was so beautiful it could never be described ... I can truly say I nearly died of excitement. One just rushed from one side of the boat to the other to see things ... [58]

Germany was entering a very dark period in its history with the Nazis in power and the great prejudice against Jews. Mary, though, was quite innocent about all this—she didn't appreciate the danger and evil throughout the country. She was focused entirely during those eighteen months on spirituality and teaching the Faith. Shoghi Effendi was delighted by her efforts and determination:

HEARTILY APPROVE CONCENTRATE PRECIOUS EFFORTS GERMANY DELIGHTED MARY'S PROGRESS LOVE[59]

Mary first met German Bahá'ís at the summer school in Esslingen in August 1935. She heard the Bahá'í prayers read in German—a language she didn't understand—and she realised that the whole world was one because even in a foreign language, she could feel the power of the Bahá'í prayers. She could really see that the Bahá'í Faith was a universal, world religion.

She learned a great deal from the German Bahá'ís that weekend including how to do without any luxury—the school was two miles up a hill that the participants had to climb in the summer heat but there was great joy so it didn't matter.

Shoghi Effendi encouraged her to help the German Bahá'ís understand the Administrative Order better so that their communities could be well-organised by local spiritual assemblies. An Assembly could organise all the community meetings like the Nineteen Day Feasts and Holy Days, encourage the teaching work, deepen the Bahá'ís, and keep unity in the community by helping Bahá'ís resolve their differences.

In those days, Bahá'í teachers who were travelling through foreign countries sent reports to Shoghi Effendi so in this way he knew what was going on in the world—there was no internet or TV in the 1930s. Mary reported to Shoghi Effendi about the problems of politics and race—Germans and Jews—that were dividing Germans under the Nazi regime. She noticed similarities between the regime and the segregation and racial prejudice in the United States:

One of the obvious problems here is that of the combination or race prejudice, fearsomeness, intense championing of the Policy & Government at present. When a Bahá'í with Jewish blood hears one without it rail against this part of his racial antecedents, it does not help the love or happiness of the community spirit ... I must say truthfully I have found more fear of almost any kind of free action among the Bahá'ís as among the other many German friends ... They say their fear of really getting busy and doing something is so that they will not jeopardize the Cause in general and I can well understand this standpoint, but even so I feel they are much more timid than is warranted from the builders of a new and Divine Order with all the power that lies behind it to be drawn upon! In other words I have no sympathy with a scared Bahá'í ... [60]

Shoghi Effendi wrote to her in response: 'I am delighted with your accomplishments. My heart is filled with hope & gratitude.'

Mary travelled on her own throughout Germany, visiting even small villages, to teach the Faith and explain the Administrative Order. She learned patience and perseverance in her service from the German Bahá'ís themselves, and she grew spiritually. When we teach the Faith, the person who learns the most is ourselves.

May and Mary continued to travel teach in Europe throughout 1936. But in that same year, the Nazis banned the Bahá'í Faith in Germany. The summer school of 1936 in Esslingen was the last nationwide gathering of the Bahá'ís of Germany. Before returning to Canada, May and Mary requested permission to come on pilgrimage, which was granted by Shoghi Effendi. They arrived in Haifa in January 1937, not knowing that their lives were about to change forever.

~

On 27 February 1937, Sutherland Maxwell got a cryptic but very important cable from his wife, May:

> *YOUR PRESENCE HERE BY MARCH TWENTY FIRST*
> *ESSENTIAL IN CONNECTION MARYS FUTURE HAPPINESS*
> *GREAT DESTINY COMPLETE SECRECY ABSOLUTELY*
> *ESSENTIAL MENTION TO NO ONE IF NECESSARY USE*
> *PRETEXT VISIT TO RANDOLPH* YOU CAN SAIL BERENGERIA*
> *ON MARCH THIRD AND CATCH TRIESTINO MARCH TENTH*
> *TRIEST ARRIVING HAIFA FIFTEENTH MAKE FLORIDA*
> *MONEY AVAILABLE CABLE REPLY OUR DEVOTED LOVE*
> *MAY*[61]

After May and Mary arrived in Haifa, Shoghi Effendi began teaching Persian to Mary. Then one day his mother brought May into a room and gave her extraordinary news. Her daughter was chosen to marry the Guardian. Mary was brought by Shoghi Effendi's younger sister into his presence. The shock to Mary of the news that she would be wed to the Guardian, who was the Sign of God on earth, must have been overwhelming.

---

* Sutherland Maxwell's brother who lived abroad.

Sutherland Maxwell received another cable on 27 February from his daughter:

My dearest daddy—Ask your consent for my marriage confirm my great happiness absolute secrecy required until after wedding and official announcement longing for your arrival bring originals Master's tablets please cable consent immediately

Your devoted loving
Mary[62]

The marriage ceremony of Shoghi Effendi and Mary Maxwell was carried out with complete simplicity. One of Shoghi Effendi's characteristics that showed his high spiritual station was his humility.

On 24 March, Shoghi Effendi drove Mary to the Tomb of Bahá'u'lláh where he chanted two prayers. Back at Abdu'l-Bahá's house, Shoghi Effendi's mother brought them into the room of the Greatest Holy Leaf where they signed the marriage certificate. Then they proceeded to the Western Pilgrim House where the Maxwells greeted the new couple.* To May, the whole event was like a dream.

Mary expressed her gratitude to her parents that day:

---

* The reason Bahá'ís were separated into Western and Eastern is because this was part of the custom of the country—to keep different cultures separate as well as men and women. The Bahá'ís were always being carefully watched by people who wanted to harm the Faith, so Bahá'ís carefully followed the customs of the land.

CHAPTER 4

My dearest, dearest ones,

On this most glorious day of my life how can I ever thank you both enough and express my love to you—for the life you gave me? For all your devotion to me; the example of your own happy marriage that gave me an ideal in life; the beauty of our home which has enriched my very soul. From you both I have woven into me so many characteristics that I hope now will be of service to the Guardian and [the] Cause.

Surely no child ever had two better, more loving parents than I! And as you have always been my pride and my dearests and my joy—so in my new life you will always continue to be!

Your own
Faithful Mary [63]

As the bride of Shoghi Effendi, Mary would now be known by a new name and title: Amatu'l-Bahá Rúhíyyih Khánum, meaning 'Handmaiden of Glory' Rúhíyyih Khánum.†

---

† 'Amatu'l-Bahá' means 'Handmaid of Glory'; 'Rúhíyyih' means 'spirit'; and 'Khánum' is the term for 'lady'.

71

Part 2

Shoghi Effendi and Rúhíyyih Khánum

Chapter 5

Marrying Shoghi Effendi was an unimaginable privilege with great life-changing responsibilities. We'll never truly know what it felt like for Rúhíyyih Khánum.

Marrying the Guardian meant that she was leaving her previous life completely behind—including all her independence—to become the wife of Shoghi Effendi with its many responsibilities and restrictions. She would be his constant companion and his helpmate in every way—most importantly assisting with huge tasks such as correspondence, managing the household, and supporting him in any way she was asked. She would have to take responsibility for the household and the endless arrangements that had to be made. She'd had a lot of practice at this in Montreal during her mother's long absences but there was one enormous difference here: The household in Haifa was Eastern in culture, not Western, like those in Canada and the United States. There was a different etiquette in the Middle East. The rules for relations between men and women were not the same. Also, they were being carefully watched by the society around them, and those who wished bad things for them.

Rúhíyyih Khánum had to learn and adapt to all these realities. And she had to learn all of this in a different language—Persian—which had a different script. Of course, she did all of this eagerly and willingly but it was still difficult for a young woman to suddenly be in such a foreign environment without any family or old friends to help her make the transition. Her letters show that she often felt lonely in those early years.

Rúhíyyih Khánum rose to the occasion, helped by the encouragement and love of Shoghi Effendi. She had never met a man like Shoghi Effendi. He was a peerless figure, a man with a great destiny whose status would only grow greater with time. He was born into a family from which flowed Divine Revelation. Raised by the loving hand and under the watchful eye of 'Abdu'l-Bahá, his upbringing was unique.

When people asked 'Abdu'l-Baha who would succeed Him, He answered:

> ... *Know verily that this is a well-guarded secret. It is even as a gem concealed within its shell. That it will be revealed is predestined. The time will come when its light will appear, when its evidences will be made manifest, and its secrets unraveled.* [64]

Shoghi Effendi, 'the well-guarded secret,' was chosen by the unfolding destiny of the Faith of Bahá'u'lláh.

'Abdu'l-Bahá wrote a letter to a Bahá'í who had asked if the new grandson who had been born to him was the child mentioned in Isaiah 11:6: 'a little child shall lead them':

Verily, that child is born and is alive and from him will appear wondrous things that thou wilt hear of in the future. Thou shall behold him endowed with the perfect appearance, supreme capacity, absolute perfection, consummate power and unsurpassed might. His face will shine with a radiance that illumines all the horizon of the world; therefore forget this not as long as thou dost live inasmuch as ages and centuries will bear traces of him. [65]

In time, 'Abdu'l-Bahá's little grandson manifested all these qualities.

Shoghi Effendi was born on 1 March 1897, in the house of Abdu'llah Pasha which the Holy Family was renting in 'Akká. They were all still prisoners of the Sultan of Turkey, and the house was right near the prison in which they had been originally kept. This is the house where the first pilgrim group from the West—the one that included Rúhíyyih Khánum's mother—was received in 1898.

From His grandson's youngest age, 'Abdu'l-Bahá insisted that Shoghi Effendi be addressed by this complete name and not just Shoghi. Effendi means 'sir', so referring to Shoghi Effendi by this full name was a sign of respect, and everyone, including family members, had to do this.

The love 'Abdu'l-Bahá had for His grandson was very deep, and this was returned by the little boy for his grandfather. Their bond was powerful and mystical. An American Bahá'í remembers this scene in 1899:

... the Beloved Master was sitting in His favourite corner of the divan ... busy writing Tablets ... Presently the Master looked up from His writing with a smile, and requested Ziyyih Khánum to chant a prayer. As she finished, a small figure appeared in the open doorway, directly opposite 'Abdu'l-Bahá. Having dropped off his shoes he stepped into the room, with his eyes focused on the Master's face. 'Abdu'l-Bahá returned his gaze with such a look of loving welcome it seemed to beckon the small one to approach him. Shoghi, that beautiful little boy, with his exquisite cameo face and his soulful appealing, dark eyes, walked slowly toward the divan, the Master drawing as by an invisible thread, until he stood quite close in front of Him. As he paused there a moment 'Abdu'l-Bahá did not offer to embrace him but sat perfectly still, only nodding his head two or three times, slowly and impressively, as if to say—'You see? This tie connecting us is not just that of a physical grandfather but something far deeper and more significant.' ... the little boy reached down and picking up the hem of 'Abdu'l-Bahá's robe he touched it reverently to his forehead, kissed it, then gently replaced it, while never taking his eyes from the adored Master's face. The next moment he turned away, and scampered off to play, like any normal child ... [66]

Shoghi Effendi was a physically small boy, but he was full of energy and was the ringleader leading the local children in pranks. He ran up and down the long flight of stairs in the house constantly, especially when he was waiting for the Master. His high spirits and exuberance sometimes worried family members as they saw the little boy rush about, up to this and that. Even Abdu'l-Bahá once wrote on a used envelope: 'Shoghi Effendi is a wise man—but he runs about very much!'[67]

Shoghi Effendi's eyes were hazel and could sometimes appear like a light-filled grey. He looked more like his great-grandfather, Bahá'u'lláh. The Greatest Holy Leaf, 'Abdu'l-Bahá's sister, took his hands once and said, 'These are like the hands of my father.'[68]

Shoghi Effendi was raised to be a polite boy. He was from both a deeply spiritual and an aristocratic family, so his manners were very refined. Towards other children, he was tender-hearted and if there ever was a problem he would embrace them before the day was over.

He was also well-disciplined. He had to be! His grandfather was 'Abdu'l-Bahá who could be strict when it came to important things. Every morning the family gathered for prayers. The children sat on the floor in the middle with their legs crossed under them and their arms folded across their chests as a mark of respect. Shoghi Effendi was always the first one there. 'Abdu'l-Bahá had reprimanded him firmly when he had been late once.

When Shoghi Effendi was five years old, 'Abdu'l-Bahá wrote him this note after the young boy kept asking to have a Tablet to him:

He is God!

O My Shoghi, I have no time to talk, leave me alone! You said 'write'—I have written. What else should be done? Now is not the time for you to read and write, it is the time for jumping about and chanting 'O My God!', therefore memorize the prayers of the Blessed Beauty and chant them that I may hear them, because there is no time for anything else. [69]

Shoghi Effendi then memorised several of Bahá'u'lláh's prayers. When 'Abdu'l-Bahá revealed a prayer for children, Shoghi Effendi was the first to chant it by heart. When he was still an infant, 'Abdu'l-Bahá asked a Muslim who chanted well at the mosque to come to His house and chant verses of the Qur'an for the baby. 'Abdu'l-Bahá and other members of the household also had beautiful voices so, as he grew up, Shoghi Effendi absorbed all these different melodies. He developed a style of chanting that was confident but had a tender and sometimes sad quality.

'Abdu'l-Bahá wanted Shoghi Effendi to be playing with friends and to be carefree while he was young. One day, Shoghi Effendi came into the Master's room and, imitating Him, he took up a pen and started to write. 'Abdu'l-Bahá brought Shoghi Effendi next to Him and said, 'Now is not the time to write, now is the time to play, you will write a lot in the future.' [70]

Shoghi Effendi loved to learn, and, though they were prisoners, the education of children could not be neglected. Classes were organised for the children of the house and taught by a Persian Bahá'í and later an Italian woman who was hired to come in as a teacher. He also was able to visit other houses in 'Akká and sometimes go with 'Abdu'l-Bahá to Bahjí which was out in the countryside. On these trips, 'Abdu'l-Bahá tucked His little grandson into bed at night.

When he slept, the little boy often had vivid dreams—sometimes reassuring and uplifting and sometimes scary. When he was an infant, he was crying one night, and 'Abdu'l-Bahá asked the nurse to bring him so he could be comforted. He said to the Greatest Holy Leaf, 'See, already he has dreams!'[71]

But though Shoghi Effendi was a young boy in 'Akká, there was great danger nearby. 'Abdu'l-Bahá's half-brother had openly opposed the position of the Master as leader of the Bahá'í community and actively worked to undermine 'Abdu'l-Bahá's authority.

Those among the Bahá'ís who followed the half-brother were declared Covenant-breakers which is someone who claims to be a Bahá'í but actively works against the head of the Bahá'í Faith. In the time of 'Abdu'l-Bahá the head of the Faith was the Master, then, after His passing, Shoghi Effendi, and today, it's the Universal House of Justice. Someone who becomes a Bahá'í but later decides to leave the Bahá'í community is not a Covenant-breaker.

Because of the Covenant-breakers, there were sudden visits by the Turkish authorities investigating 'Abdu'l-Bahá on false charges, threats on His life, and the possibility of His being sent into exile in Libya. This created a lot of anxiety among the members of the Holy Family. The danger around them was very real: 'Abdu'l-Bahá had to warn Shoghi Effendi when he was very young not to drink coffee in any of the homes he visited because of the danger of poisoning.

Chapter 6

When Shoghi Effendi was an older boy he entered the Jesuit school in Haifa, then he attended a Catholic school in Beirut and finally the Syrian Protestant College in Beirut. In those days no one had surnames so 'Abdu'l-Bahá gave him the name 'Rabbani' which meant 'divine' so that he would not be confused with his cousins who had the name 'Afnan'.

Shoghi Effendi was not happy at any of these schools. His background was so different from those of the other students that he stood quite apart. With his sensitive and open-hearted nature, this must have been difficult for him. He also greatly missed the presence of his Grandfather. He spent all his vacations in Haifa with Him. His only real desire in life was to serve Him.

'Abdu'l-Bahá left Palestine in 1910 for the first time in forty years. He was finally a free man and decided that He would travel to the West—Europe and America—and teach the Faith.

The first stop was Egypt because from there, ocean liners went to the West. Shoghi Effendi was with Him and learned an important lesson in Egypt. 'Abdu'l-Bahá, the young Shoghi Effendi, and an important guest were being driven to the city of Ramleh near Alexandria in Egypt. At the end of the ride, the driver demanded an exorbitantly high price. 'Abdu'l-Bahá refused to pay this price because it was unjust. The driver grabbed and shook the Master to the great shock and embarrassment of the little boy who had never seen anyone treat his grandfather like this. But 'Abdu'l-Bahá remained calm. Finally the driver took the correct price for the fare. The Master told him that the driver had lost the good tip He had planned to give him. When he grew into a man, Shoghi Effendi followed 'Abdu'l-Bahá's example and never allowed himself to be cheated by anyone.

In March 1912, 'Abdu'l-Bahá undertook His historic journey to the West. The young Shoghi Effendi must have been beyond excited to be with his Grandfather out on the seas in a big boat travelling to the unknown West to spread the message of Bahá'u'lláh. But when the boat docked in Italy, the authorities told Shoghi Effendi and two of the other Bahá'ís they could not land and would have to go back because they had eye infections. This was not true. It was a lie circulated by jealous people around 'Abdu'l-Bahá.

Shoghi Effendi was heartbroken. He had the opportunity to be with his Grandfather on this extremely exciting and history-making trip only to have it stolen from him. Like the many disappointments he would have later in his life, he accepted it and returned to Egypt.

Shoghi Effendi followed this trip throughout the West as best he could by reading the talks of 'Abdu'l-Bahá that were printed in the Bahá'í publication, *The Star of the West*. He drew a detailed map of the United States to follow the journey of his Grandfather.

World War I broke out in 1914, and there were terrible difficulties in the Holy Land. The region was completely cut-off from the rest of the world, food was running out, and the Allied armies bombed Haifa. 'Abdu'l-Bahá and His family moved to a village in the foothills for protection; Shoghi Effendi was most likely with them. The governor of 'Akká at the time was a cruel man who hated the Bahá'ís. He planned to take advantage of the confusion of the war to have 'Abdu'l-Bahá crucified. This plan did not come to fruition because the British armies entered Haifa two days before the planned date.

After returning from school in Beirut in 1918, Shoghi Effendi spent the next two years shadowing 'Abdu'l-Bahá. He went to many public gatherings with Him and was able to observe how 'Abdu'l-Bahá treated with the same respect and attention people from all backgrounds. He also took on a great deal of the correspondence for the Master. By 1920 it was decided Shoghi Effendi would attend Oxford University in England. There were several others who could now help with correspondence and so the time was right. The Master was in excellent health. So much so, in fact, that he began speaking of making a teaching trip to India, Japan, Hawaii, and back through the United States!

In His *Will and Testament*, 'Abdu'l-Bahá described Shoghi Effendi in exalted terms.

Shoghi Effendi was 'the blest and sacred bough that hath branched out from the Twin Holy Trees,' whose shade 'shadoweth all mankind;'

'the Sign of God, the chosen branch, the Guardian of the Cause of God.'[72]

The young boy 'Abdu'l-Bahá had cared for, protected, and trained, had grown into a young man capable of being the Guardian of the Bahá'í Faith. The Master had known of his capacity all along.

But for Shoghi Effendi, losing 'Abdu'l-Bahá's presence in this world left him for years with a sense of abandonment and a great longing for what he could never have again—the reassuring presence, love, and guidance of the Master.

When Shoghi Effendi became the Guardian of the Bahá'í Faith, all the challenges the Master had faced now confronted him. He would have to dig deep into his soul to come up with the strength to be the Guardian of the Bahá'í Faith.

Shoghi Effendi rose heroically to the challenge. He became the unfailing guide and general for all Bahá'ís. Thanks to him, the Bahá'í community went from existing in only a few countries to becoming a world religion.

But in 1921, the time of 'Abdu'l-Bahá's passing, Shoghi Effendi was only twenty-four years old when he was suddenly made responsible for the entire Bahá'í community and its progress. Everyone looked to him now! But many older Bahá'ís wondered about such a young man being in charge, and they expected Shoghi Effendi to organise the election of the Universal House of Justice which would be an institution with experienced older Bahá'ís on it instead of one lone young man. According to 'Abdu'l-Bahá's *Will and Testament*, His twin successors were the Guardian and the Universal House of Justice, the latter having been ordained by Bahá'u'lláh in His Most Holy Book.

But the faithful believers soon realised the great wisdom of Shoghi Effendi's appointment. For example, Mr Asgarzadeh* was an experienced Bahá'í who went to England to assist Shoghi Effendi during his university days. When he heard the news of the Master's passing, he decided he should return to Haifa to assist the Holy Family with all the work and details to prepare for the election of the Universal House of Justice. In Haifa, he learned that this young man, Shoghi Effendi, whom he had just been assisting in England was now the Guardian of the Faith. He had a crisis of faith—he felt the entire world had fallen in on him! It had to be a test and couldn't be true.

On his way to Haifa, Mr Asgarzadeh was going over in his mind the steps that should take place to elect the Universal House of Justice. It made most sense to him that each large national Bahá'í community would choose one person to serve on the Universal House of Justice. He started with his home community of Ashghabat, a very large Bahá'í community at the time. That was an easy choice: Siyyid Golpaygani was the elder most respected Bahá'í there. Then he realised that Golpaygani would be serving with Bahá'ís from the West, and he didn't speak any of their languages. So he went down the list of other Bahá'ís in Ashgabat but none had the stature or the linguistic abilities. Then he thought to himself that the Faith had no boundaries so Ashgabat could choose anyone from the Bahá'í world to be its

---

* This story was told by Professor Amin Banani in a talk in 2003.

representative on the House of Justice. So who could be Ashgabat's representative? Well, Shoghi Effendi spoke all the languages, and he could serve. Then he thought about the large communities in Persia. They had many deepened, older Bahá'ís but none really had the international qualifications. He said to himself that there was no rule that a representative could only be for one country, so Shoghi Effendi could also represent Persia. He went through this same process and each community only had Shoghi Effendi who was suitable. Suddenly he realised that, of course, 'Abdu'l-Bahá knew what He was doing. Mr Asgarzadeh accepted that Shoghi Effendi was the best person to connect the whole Bahá'í world.

When he arrived in Haifa, the Greatest Holy Leaf greeted him and said that he was just in time to help because Shoghi Effendi had so much to do. Shoghi Effendi then came in and after embracing him, pulled out a copy of the *Will and Testament* and said that multiple copies had to be made to send out to Bahá'í communities. Asgarzadeh sat and read the *Will* for the first time and was overwhelmed by the language 'Abdu'l-Bahá used to describe Shoghi Effendi. As he copied the document by hand, tears flowed from his eyes and ruined several copies. He was now convinced of the truth of the Guardianship.

Shoghi Effendi summoned experienced Bahá'ís from different communities to come to Haifa and consult on what the next steps should be for the development of the Bahá'í world. Many of these Bahá'ís initially thought the best thing to do would be to bring the Universal House of Justice into existence. The Governor in Haifa told one of them that the House of Justice should be created so that all the

Bahá'í holy properties in the region could be given over to this institution and not the Covenant-breakers from 'Abdu'l-Bahá's family.

But Shoghi Effendi, even at twenty-four, knew better than all of them. He had the bigger vision of the future that they did not have. The Universal House of Justice was like a magnificent stone roof. It had to be built on strong pillars and walls. Those were the Local and National Assemblies. In 1921, there were too few Assemblies, and the Bahá'ís did not understand the role of these institutions much at all. During the Master's life, they were all devoted to 'Abdu'l-Bahá. Now, under Shoghi Effendi, they would set about creating an Administrative Order centred on Spiritual Assemblies to which they would turn for guidance. These Assemblies would become the strong pillars upon which the Universal House of Justice would be established.

Soon, Bahá'ís all came to trust 'Abdu'l-Bahá's words and see that Shoghi Effendi, despite his young age, was eminently qualified to be the Guardian of the Bahá'í Faith, that he was the 'sign of God on earth.'

Chapter 7

When he became the Guardian, Shoghi Effendi's heart and mind were in turmoil. He grieved the loss of 'Abdu'l-Bahá intensely. He had all these new responsibilities and challenges that appeared to be well-beyond what one person could do. The strain was almost overwhelming for his body—when the doctor tested his nerves by tapping his knee, there was no reaction. Shoghi Effendi needed to go and spend a long time in nature to restore his health.

Shoghi Effendi did his healing in the Swiss Alps, the tallest mountains in Europe. He rented a small room in an attic that had a bed and a basin and pitcher of cold water for washing. He got up before dawn and walked for miles in the mountains in the bright sunshine and pure air. He had to conquer himself. He could no longer be Shoghi Effendi, the young Persian man who had grown up in Palestine and gone to school in Beirut and Oxford, he had to *become* the Guardian, not just have the title. He had to forget about himself.

Returning to Haifa with his strength renewed, Shoghi Effendi faced the many challenges of being Guardian with determination and faith. He would need both. No challenge was greater than the attacks of the Covenant-breakers. After 'Abdu'l-Bahá's passing, several prominent Bahá'ís opposed Shoghi Effendi. They were jealous of him and wanted leadership for themselves. They didn't understand that Shoghi Effendi was the leader of the Bahá'í Faith but he wasn't a leader like a king or president. He was a servant.

Servitude is the highest position a human being can reach.

Shoghi Effendi did not see himself as superior to other Bahá'ís and always referred to himself as their brother and co-worker in the Cause. He never spent the money of the Bahá'í funds on himself such as buying many clothes, cars, or travelling in first class even though he could have. But Covenant-breakers often did see themselves as superior. This was their ego which had become sick.

For Shoghi Effendi, the most painful of all Covenant-breaking was when members of 'Abdu'l-Bahá's family and his own turned against him as the Guardian. We expect our family members to care for us, ask us if they can help, listen to us when we need to talk, and help us in times of need. The members of his family did the opposite. Gradually Shoghi Effendi came to be almost totally alone except for the Greatest Holy Leaf and later, Rúhíyyih Khánum. She remembers during her pilgrimage with her mother in 1923 that Shoghi Effendi called them in to his room where he lay in his bed with deep circles under his eyes saying he could not stand this anymore.

Rúhíyyih Khánum wrote in her diary that the effects of Covenant-breaking on Shoghi Effendi were like '... a man in a blizzard who cannot sometimes even open his eyes for the blinding snow,' and '... a man whose skin has been burned off ...'[73] and that even time could not remove the scars of it.[74] Shoghi Effendi gave every chance to Covenant-breakers to change, he often spoke with them at great length even imploring them if they were family members.

While Shoghi Effendi's letters are written in very formal language and can sometimes seem stern, he had a very sensitive nature. When he knew a Bahá'í was having a tough time or suffering, he cabled them with a message of love. He was considerate and thorough in caring for others. When a lady had difficulties trying to return home from pilgrimage, he sent seven cables trying to help her. When an American Bahá'í became very ill coming back from Iran, he cabled Bahá'í communities to meet them at their ship and take care of them. When he was in Switzerland, he made sure to take a train to the grave of a Bahá'í pioneer to pray for him.

He also could have a sense of humour like 'Abdu'l-Bahá, sometimes even laughing out loud or teasing family members and Rúhíyyih Khánum. She usually fell for it when he was teasing her because he could be a very good actor.

After 'Abdu'l-Bahá, Shoghi Effendi's deepest human relationship was with his great-aunt Bahiyyih Khánum, the Greatest Holy Leaf. Once he became the Guardian, he was the focus of her life. She watched over him with great care and concern. He ate his one meal a day with her in her room. During those times, she could see his condition and would counsel him. He kept photos of her all over his room. In his early correspondence he included her in his signing off, writing 'the Greatest Holy Leaf and I' or referring to 'we' and 'us'.

When Shoghi Effendi so suddenly became Guardian, and he 'ceased to be a normal human being,'[75] it was the Greatest Holy

Leaf alone who held the Bahá'í community together while he went to Switzerland to recover. In the last years of her life, her eyesight and strength faded but she must have taken great joy in seeing the strong person Shoghi Effendi grew into as the Guardian, knowing the Faith was secure in his hands. When she passed away in 1932, Shoghi Effendi described her death as the 'sudden removal of my sole earthly sustainer, the joy and solace of my life.' He cabled to the Bahá'í world to suspend all Bahá'í festivities as an act of bereavement because she was the 'last remnant of Bahá'u'lláh.' [76]

After her passing, his great helpmate became Rúhíyyih Khánum.

Chapter 8

Shoghi Effendi married Rúhíyyih Khánum in a very simple ceremony like that of 'Abdu'l-Bahá. The marriage took place with no advance notice because Shoghi Effendi knew that any big event would draw unwanted attention to the Bahá'ís in Haifa. So the servants in the house were surprised when the car drove Shoghi Effendi and the young Canadian lady to the Shrine of Bahá'u'lláh on the afternoon of 25 March 1937.

Rúhíyyih Khánum dressed in black. This was the custom in that part of the world. Shoghi Effendi wanted Rúhíyyih Khánum to fit into the culture of the household which was Middle Eastern. While she had grown up in a very different culture, she was more than happy to do as Shoghi Effendi wished.

The couple entered the Shrine. Shoghi Effendi asked his bride for the ring which she had been wearing hidden around her neck. He placed the ring on her right hand's ring finger. Then he stepped into the inner shrine under which Bahá'u'lláh's body was interred. He picked up dried rose petals with a handkerchief that the keeper of the Shrine always put in a silver bowl at the feet of Bahá'u'lláh. Shoghi Effendi chanted the Tablet of Visitation. The couple returned to Haifa and had the marriage ceremony in the room formerly lived in by the Greatest Holy Leaf. His parents signed the marriage certificate showing that they gave their consent to the union.

Rúhíyyih Khánum then went to Western Pilgrim House to be with her parents. Because of the culture of Palestine, the Eastern pilgrims and the Western pilgrims were kept in separate houses. At dinner time, Shoghi Effendi joined them. He took out the handkerchief and unfolded it with a warm smile and gave May Maxwell the petals telling her they were from the Holy Shrine of Bahá'u'lláh. Rúhíyyih Khánum's parents then signed the marriage certificate showing their consent. After dinner, Shoghi Effendi and Rúhíyyih Khánum went off together to the home of 'Abdu'l-Bahá where he had his rooms.

A message was sent out to the Bahá'í world about their marriage. Shoghi Effendi wanted his marriage with Rúhíyyih Khánum to be seen by Bahá'ís as the union of East and West: 'Emphasize significance institution Guardianship union East West and linking destinies Persia America.'[77] When 'Abdu'l-Bahá and Shoghi Effendi used the terms East they meant Persia and the Near East, and when they used the term West they meant the Americas and Europe. It was extremely rare for people to travel outside their countries or marry people from other countries. A person would have to travel for weeks to get from Persia to North America and almost no one other than Bahá'ís made this trip. A marriage with people from the East and West—Shoghi Effendi was Persian and Rúhíyyih Khánum was Canadian—symbolised the unity of the world which is the fundamental teaching of the Faith.*

Through her marriage, Rúhíyyih Khánum's parents became family to Shoghi Effendi. He grew much closer to them as members of his own family turned against the Guardianship. May Maxwell, whose only desire was to serve the Cause and Shoghi Effendi, died of a heart attack while on a trip to Argentina. He broke the news to Rúhíyyih Khánum. She remembered the great kindness with which he did it and how he'd comforted her during that difficult period. He made her happy when he described to her that May Maxwell was going around the Abhá Kingdom talking about how wonderful her dear daughter was.

After May Maxwell's passing, Shoghi Effendi and Sutherland Maxwell became much closer and began to work together on projects including the design of the Shrine of the Báb. Eventually Sutherland Maxwell made his main home in Haifa. Shoghi Effendi greatly valued his friendship and his talent for architecture, a subject that interested Shoghi Effendi and for which he had an excellent eye. It must have been an extraordinary joy for Rúhíyyih Khánum to have her father— whom she referred to as 'dad'—with them in Haifa.

---

* Today the terms 'East' and 'West' are no longer used as much. Since the words are directions, anywhere that is east of you is East and west of you is West. Today when someone uses the term 'Far East' they mean China, Japan, Korea, and Taiwan, and Persia—today Iran—is usually described as being in the 'Middle East' but all these terms are relative to where your own country is on earth.

Being the Guardian was extremely difficult. Rúhíyyih Khánum became Shoghi Effendi's main helpmate. She kept a diary of her time with Shoghi Effendi. In many of the entries, she expresses how hard life was for Shoghi Effendi because of the amount of work he had, the lack of enough people to help, and the difficulties other members of his family gave him. She wrote in 1943:

Anyone who knew the true story of Shoghi Effendi's life would weep—weep for his goodness, weep for his pure, simple heart, weep for his labours and his cares, weep for the long, long years in which he has toiled ever more alone ... [78]

She had to watch someone she loved suffer greatly:

He forces himself to go on and finish the letters he has had piled for days on his desk—but he reads a thing sometimes ten minutes over and over because he can't concentrate! I think no suffering is worse than seeing someone you love suffer. And I can't remedy it. [79]

Rúhíyyih Khánum was extremely loyal and endured everything with him, nursing him when he was ill:

He says he feels like a broken reed. No doubt partly due to his having been very ill for ten days with an awful fever ... I have nursed him day and night and to say we have been through a kind of hell is no exaggeration. To be alone with the Guardian

so ill … was such a strain and a responsibility! I think we slept
at most 4 hours a night for a week![80]

Making it more difficult for the two of them were the dangers of
World War II and the violence of the Arab-Israeli conflict after
the War.

In 1940, as the War broke out, Shoghi Effendi had to make a trip to
England. Rúhíyyih Khánum's mother had just died in Argentina, and
her father, who was in poor health, had come to live in Haifa. They
tried to get visas to England. With all the turmoil of the War, these
were hard to get. When they absolutely had to leave if they wanted to
make it to England in time, the visas had not yet been granted. Shoghi
Effendi decided that they would leave for Italy anyway, hoping they'd
get visas there. The three left the Bay of Haifa on an old aquaplane
which is a plane that takes off on water using propellers. Water was
sloshing around the old boards on the bottom of the plane.

They arrived in Rome a few days later. Rúhíyyih Khánum and
her father went to the British Consul for Shoghi Effendi to see about
getting visas. They were told that this was impossible because the
Consul didn't have the authority to issue them, and he couldn't get
in touch with headquarters in London because the War had cut the
communications. When they gave the bad news to Shoghi Effendi, he
told them to go back and try again. Though Rúhíyyih Khánum could
not see what the point was of going back, she did as Shoghi Effendi
asked because he was the Guardian after all. Back in the office of the
Consul, Rúhíyyih Khánum mentioned that Shoghi Effendi was the

successor to 'Abdu'l-Bahá. The Consul had known 'Abdu'l-Bahá in the Holy Land and recounted a memory about the Master which had moved him very much. He stamped visas into their passports. He said that because he didn't have the authority to do that, they were worthless but might help them get into England.

Rúhíyyih Khánum always felt that the presence of Shoghi Effendi was opening the way:

> It does not seem real at all that war has come to the world. Passing through blackened towns—seeing troop trains moving up—waiting to hear the radio news … Shoghi Effendi's way has been opened as it always will be—the scene seemed to crash behind us, but we were safely through. [81]

A few days after the travellers left Italy, that country joined the war. The travellers went by train through all of France. Rúhíyyih Khánum was disturbed by what she saw:

> It is hard to describe the period that followed. The whole episode was like a brilliantly lit nightmare—a personal nightmare for us and a giant nightmare in which the whole of Europe was involved. As our train made its way to Paris every station was crowded with thousands of refugees fleeing the rapidly crumbling Allied front in the North. There was no way of getting any accurate information, chaos was descending. [82]

The tired travellers made it to Paris where they found out that no more boats were going to England. The only chance they had was to go to the small port city of St. Malo nearby and see if they could catch one there. Hundreds of people trying to get to England flooded the small town.

Shoghi Effendi, Rúhíyyih Khánum, and Sutherland Maxwell, waited for days for signs of a boat. Rúhíyyih Khánum observed that Shoghi Effendi sat for hours like a statue. She felt that he was suffering greatly. She knew that if the Nazis overtook them, Shoghi Effendi would be in real trouble because the grand Mufti in Jerusalem, the capital of Palestine, hated the Bahá'í Faith and allied himself with the Nazis. Finally a ship arrived. The travellers made it to England. The next day, the Nazis entered Saint-Malo.

When it came time to return to Palestine, the travellers were able to get visas because Sutherland Maxwell knew the Canadian High Commissioner in London.

At that time, the boats were full as the British were evacuating children to safety from the approaching Nazis. They left just in time. The Nazi and British air forces and navies fought one another in the Battle of Britain. Beginning in September, the Nazis bombed English cities for 56 out of 57 days in a row. Forty thousand innocent civilians were killed, and a million homes destroyed.

The boat went south along the coast of Africa. This was the only available route open to them. The boat zig-zagged in the water to avoid submarines trying to sink it. The travellers debarked in Cape Town all the way at the Southern end of the African continent. Sutherland was not feeling well at all. Now they would have to travel overland across the entire continent. Shoghi Effendi was worried about Sutherland Maxwell's health and recommended he stay in Durban for a while rather than undertake the overland route, which was going to be difficult. He could then proceed by other ways to Palestine and wait for them in a hotel in Nazareth.

Shoghi Effendi and Rúhíyyih Khánum set out for Cairo which was all the way on the northern coast of the continent. They drove over bumpy roads through the Congo, which is most of central Africa, 5,000 miles to the city of Juba in the Sudan. There, they boarded a boat and went down the Nile to Khartoum, Sudan, which Rúhíyyih Khánum described as the hottest place on earth. In the evening, they were sitting on the porch of their hotel in Khartoum when a group of airline passengers stepped up. Among them was Rúhíyyih Khánum's father who had just flown there!

The travellers arrived back in Haifa six months after they had left. The war intensified. The Nazi armies were approaching the Middle East and getting ready to invade. During 1941, Shoghi Effendi worried greatly about the approach of the war and what to do. If the Nazis arrived in Palestine, the Grand Mufti would surely turn them against the Bahá'ís, whose beliefs were so contrary to their own.

There were regular blackouts of electricity when everyone had to live in the dark at night. Bomb sirens went off. A few bombs fell nearby. But Palestine was not taken by the Nazis. One day, though, as Shoghi Effendi was writing the great history of the Bahá'í Faith, *God Passes By*, 'two army fighter planes in practice flight touched wings, lost control and crashed, one coming down over the roof of our house so low I thought it would sheer through the ceiling of

Shoghi Effendi's room. It landed and burst into flames not 100 yards away at the foot of the street.'[83]

In the years after World War II, Palestine broke out into civil war between Arabs and Jews over control of the land. Jewish refugees were arriving to settle in Palestine in increasingly larger numbers. In Europe they had been the victims of the Holocaust, the Nazi effort to kill all the Jews in Europe. They were coming to Palestine to establish a homeland where Jewish people could protect themselves. The new arrivals came into conflict with the Palestinian Arabs who were already living there. This violence engulfed Haifa where Shoghi Effendi and Rúhíyyih Khánum lived:

Where once a gun shot would have made our blood run cold and filled you with indignation, you soon, from endless repetition, just get used to it ... and go on about your business. Later you hear who and how was shot by these bullets.[84]

Gladys will now sleep over at this house ... so we can have her near us as the shooting is too much for her to be all alone in the Pilgrim House at night ... Besides it is dangerous for anyone to come and go across the street after dark ...*[85]

The battle itself was constant and real war. That night for me it was like sleeping at the bottom of a stagnant pool which someone was constantly stirring. I was so tired I did sleep sometimes, but then dream and firing and bombs became all

---

* Gladys Anderson was a Bahá'í who was serving the Guardian in Haifa with her husband, Ben.

one torpid mixture which was almost worse than sleeping or waking.[86]

To prevent acts of terrorism, street lights were often turned out at night, making everything dark and frightening:

As the terrorism increased, certain areas, including our own, were voluntarily blacked out at night with no street lights at all; they were often day-time curfews imposed, when pitched battles or major acts of terrorism took place and only the British forces moved about, their great tanks howling down the abandoned streets, often firing random bursts from their machine guns as they rolled by. The wailing noise of their sirens was a most eerie, unpleasant sound, but at night, it was really terrifying to an already nerve-wracked population living on the edge of a volcano which might explode any time.[87]

Despite the terrible difficulties in the world during the 1930s and 40s, Shoghi Effendi did not stop guiding Bahá'ís. He kept up a stream of writing—letters, very long letters published as books later, and *God Passes By.* His writing helped Bahá'ís to have a hopeful view of the future. Even though the world was at war, it will eventually achieve the Lesser Peace when warfare between countries will generally cease. Then the peoples of the world will acknowledge the claims of Bahá'u'lláh, and the Bahá'í Faith will spiritualise the body of humanity.

Chapter 9

Shoghi Effendi loved words. He was very precise about his choice of words so that his writing would say exactly what he meant.

Rúhíyyih Khánum almost always sat with him when he wrote so she could be of assistance when he wanted it. He frequently asked her to pass him the enormous dictionary he used to look up words.

Shoghi Effendi wrote in a very 'high' style, not like the language you read in a magazine or social media article which is simpler, more like the way people speak every day. For many readers, the vocabulary he chose was difficult, requiring strong reading skills. Why didn't Shoghi Effendi write in a simpler style, more the way we speak?

His language had to match his exalted position of Guardian of the Bahá'í Faith; imagine if he wore shorts and a t-shirt instead of proper clothes when he met people. This would look very odd and inappropriate to guests expecting to meet the Head of the Bahá'í Faith. Also, he was not just writing to people in his day but also for people living hundreds of years in the future. Bahá'ís will always read the writings of Shoghi Effendi and look to them for guidance. Language that is precise and elevated will last longer because everyday language changes all the time. If you want to build a house that lasts, it's better to build it in stone rather than wood.

We must read the writings of Shoghi Effendi to gain a deeper understanding of the Bahá'í Faith and its place in history.

Shoghi Effendi wrote thousands of pages during his time as the Guardian. Much of his writing consisted of letters he wrote in response to Bahá'ís who had questions for him. Bahá'ís all over the world asked him for personal advice—where they should go to college, whether they should marry, where they should go pioneer for the Bahá'í Faith, how they should best serve the Faith and many other questions. Over the years a few people close to him such as Rúhíyyih Khánum would help him with this type of correspondence.

As Head of the Bahá'í Faith, he had to guide the Bahá'í community. He made plans for it to grow such as the Seven-Year Plan and the Ten-Year Crusade, among others. These could be quite detailed. Shoghi Effendi kept track of all the progress of the goals using charts and maps.

Additionally, he explained to Bahá'ís the role of the Faith in history and in the events that were unfolding all around them. The Great Depression and World War II—the 1930s and 40s—were years of terrible upheaval and violence.

To help Bahá'ís understand the progress of the Faith and the great tests they were experiencing, he wrote long letters which were the length of short books and are published today in book form.

In 1929, he wrote *The World Order of Bahá'u'lláh* to explain the nature and purpose of the Administrative Order, a structure which came directly from the Writings of Bahá'u'lláh. Bahá'í institutions should be like channels through which the spirit of the Faith can reach the world. The Bahá'í Administrative Order has a purpose, which is to release spirit into the world and create more unity and understanding using the Teachings of Bahá'u'lláh.

In 1931, Shoghi Effendi sent out his next major letter to the Bahá'ís of the West, *The Goal of a New World Order*. These were the years after World War I but before World War II when there was a lot of anxiety that Europe would slide into open warfare again. Several European countries had colonies on other continents so another war would draw in many other parts of the world as well. Shoghi Effendi explained that the world system of Bahá'u'lláh was the solution.

The next year, 1932, Shoghi Effendi wrote a letter later published as "The Golden Age of the Cause of Bahá'u'lláh" in which he emphasises that the Bahá'í Faith is divine in origin, not a movement that has sprung out from this world. He explains in this letter some uniquely Bahá'í concepts:

> *Its teachings revolve around the fundamental principle that religious truth is not absolute but relative, that Divine Revelation is progressive, not final. Unequivocally and without the least reservation it proclaims all established religions to be divine in origin, identical in their aims, complementary in their functions, continuous in their purpose, indispensable in their value to mankind.* [88]

The Bahá'í teaching is that all religions are one because they all *come from God*. It is not that religions are all equally good but different—they are, in their essence, the same religion, the Religion of God.

Religion is *progressive* because God has always made Himself known through His Manifestations and will continue to do so in the future. Every age has different needs. Today the world needs unity to deal with climate change and other challenges. In the time of cavemen, the idea of world unity would not have made any sense as they were concerned only with hunting and gathering and surviving.

Because the purpose of the Bahá'í Faith is world unity, Shoghi Effendi warned Bahá'ís not to become involved with political parties. The Bahá'í way is to work constructively with governments, organisations, and individuals for the betterment of society, to engage in non-partisan consultation to solve problems, and to promote understanding between individuals. Partisanship does the opposite—it turns people against one another.

In 1934, he wrote a letter later published as "The Dispensation of Bahá'u'lláh" which 'burst upon the Bahá'ís like a blinding white light' as Rúhíyyih Khánum remembers. She describes reading it for the first time:

> *I remember when I first read it I had the most extraordinary feeling as if the whole universe had suddenly expanded around me and I was looking out into its dazzling star-filled immensity; all the frontiers of our understanding flew outwards; the glory of this Cause and the true station of its Central Figures were revealed to us and we were never the same again.*[89]

Shoghi Effendi wrote "The Dispensation of Bahá'u'lláh" to explain to explain the stations of the Central Figures. The Báb was both the

Herald of the Bahá'í Faith—meaning the person who came before to prepare the way—and a Manifestation of God who revealed His own Holy Book, the *Bayan*, and His own Laws. Bahá'u'lláh is the Supreme Manifestation of God meaning he is the One promised by the religions of the past. The Báb ended the Cycle of Prophecy which began many thousands of years ago. Prophecies pointed to Bahá'u'lláh who began a new Cycle during which we will see the unity of humanity. 'Abdu'l-Bahá was not a Manifestation of God like the Báb and Bahá'u'lláh. Many early Bahá'ís in the West thought 'Abdu'l-Bahá was the Return of Jesus Christ. The Master was the Centre of the Covenant meaning that all Bahá'ís had to follow Him and his interpretations of the Bahá'í Writings after the passing of Bahá'u'lláh. He was also not an ordinary man; he was inspired by the Holy Spirit and led a perfect life. He gave us an example of how to live that we must try to imitate, so one of His titles is the 'Perfect Exemplar'.

Anyone who wants to understand the basics of the Bahá'í beliefs about the Báb, Bahá'u'lláh, 'Abdu'l-Bahá and the Administrative Order, must read "The Dispensation of Bahá'u'lláh".

In 1936, Shoghi Effendi wrote "The Unfoldment of World Civilization", a letter in which he gave Bahá'ís a vision of the glorious future ahead. A new world order based on the Teachings of Bahá'u'lláh will be rolled out while the old one crumbles:

The earth will be governed by a world federal government consisting of central and national governments.

This stage would mark 'the coming of age of the entire human race.'[90]

Shoghi Effendi spent countless hours, day after day, month after month hunched over a small typewriter. Before computers, typewriters had to be used; if you made a mistake you would have to hand-correct it or retype the page. Your back, wrists, arms, and eyes would all become very tired. The constant writing was painful for Shoghi Effendi.

In addition to these major letters and the constant personal letters from Bahá'ís, Shoghi Effendi also undertook one of the most difficult forms of writing: translation. What makes translating so difficult is that in addition to finding the right word to match the one in the original language, you also must capture the meaning, the mood, and the connotations from the original language. Many languages have terms and ideas that cannot be translated into English. The original Bahá'í Writings are all in Persian and Arabic. Shoghi Effendi had to capture in English the beauty and majesty and ideas in the original Arabic and Persian. This is an extremely challenging task because there are many choices of words to be made, and Arabic and Persian have words with meanings that are not found in English. Fortunately, Shoghi Effendi had mastered these three languages.

His first major translation was the *Book of Certitude*, the *Kitáb-i-Iqán*, the second most important book revealed by Bahá'u'lláh. This book was revealed in response to questions from the uncle of the Báb about the Station of the Báb. In it, Bahá'u'lláh shows how religion is progressive by explaining how the prophecies of Christianity and Islam had been fulfilled by the Báb.

His next translation project was the *Dawn-Breakers*, a chronicle of the times of the Báb and the early Bahá'í Faith by Nabil-i-Zarandi. A chronicle is written by someone who lived *through* the events they are writing about. It is a mixture of what they saw first-hand and what they heard from others at the time. Nabil lived through the events during the life of the Báb and Bahá'u'lláh. His chronicle contains a lot of very valuable information and accounts.

Shoghi Effendi assembled the original papers of Nabil that were in Persian, and he brought them together to create a consistent story. He researched the events described in *The Dawn-Breakers* to check facts and fill in gaps as much as possible. He also sent a photographer to go around Iran and take pictures of the many historical and holy places where the events of the early Bábí and Bahá'í Faiths took place. He included a detailed genealogy of the Báb's family. Most precious of all, he had the original tablets which the Báb wrote to the Letters of the Living reproduced in full colour. He had 300 formal editions made with all of these included—the footnotes, the photos, and the tablets.

Shoghi Effendi took this much care and effort because Nabil's chronicle gives a first-hand view of the early history of the Faith, and he wanted Bahá'ís in the West to know this history. He often referred to American Bahá'ís as the descendants of the figures in the Dawn-Breakers who were so courageous. He wanted the Bahá'ís of the West to show this same courage in teaching the Bahá'í Faith.

This enormous project took Shoghi Effendi two years. He dedicated it to his great aunt, the Greatest Holy Leaf, the person he loved the most after his Grandfather. At the end of it he wrote to a Bahá'í, 'I am so overcome with fatigue caused by the long and severe strain of the work I have undertaken that I must stop and lie down.'[91]

His next translation project was titled *Gleanings from the Writings of Bahá'u'lláh* which was published in 1935. Very few of Bahá'u'lláh's Writings had been translated by that time. He wanted Bahá'ís to know and understand much more of the Bahá'í Writings. Bahá'u'lláh wrote over a hundred volumes of books, tablets, poems, and prayers. Shoghi Effendi could read them all and chose passages from among them for *Gleanings* that he felt were especially important for Bahá'ís to know and essential to understanding the Bahá'í Faith.

Even though today many more books of Bahá'u'lláh have been translated, reading and studying *Gleanings* is still very important because Shoghi Effendi selected these as among the essential passages for Bahá'ís to know—and no one knew better than him!

Next, Shoghi Effendi translated prayers by Bahá'u'lláh and these were published as *Prayers and Meditations*. He included in this book the work by Bahá'u'lláh called *The Hidden Words*. *The Hidden Words* are made up of very short passages, which Bahá'u'lláh explains are the core teachings of all the religions of the world.

The last major translation project Shoghi Effendi undertook was Bahá'u'lláh's *Epistle to the Son of the Wolf*. The epistle was Bahá'u'lláh's last major work of revelation. Much of it is Him quoting from his earlier works so, while it was a letter to a cleric who had been cruel towards Bahá'ís, it contains several fundamental teachings of the Faith. Shoghi Effendi thought that Bahá'ís would be assisted in their service by knowing the verities contained in the *Epistle to the Son of the Wolf.*

For most people all the above writings would be enough for an entire lifetime but Shoghi Effendi had more to come!

In 1939, because of the violence in Palestine, he wrote a letter later published as *The Advent of Divine Justice* while he was living in Europe. *The Advent of Divine Justice* was written to the Bahá'ís of the United States and Canada and explained to them their role in the development of the Bahá'í Faith around the world within the Seven-Year Plan, which been launched two years earlier. 'Abdu'l-Bahá had written the Tablets of the Divine Plan to the Bahá'ís of North America calling on them to arise and serve the Faith around the world. The first Seven-Year Plan was the first organised effort to fulfil the Divine Plan of 'Abdu'l-Bahá. Two of its main goals were for Spiritual Assemblies to be established in each state of the United States and country of Latin America.

In the *Advent of Divine Justice*, Shoghi Effendi contrasted the greatness of the Teachings of Bahá'u'lláh with the social conditions of North America which he criticised for its poor morals, political corruption, materialism, and racism—which he described as 'the most vital and challenging issue.' Everyone, he said, had a responsibility to eliminate these social ills.

In the second year of World War II, Shoghi Effendi wrote a letter later published as *The Promised Day is Come* to the Bahá'ís of North

America and Europe. In very strong language, Shoghi Effendi writes that the ills of the world are due to the rejection of the Manifestation of God by human beings.

World War II caused the death of more than eighty million people, and its effects caused many more millions to perish. It was the bloodiest war in human history. Shoghi Effendi's message was that the remedy for the problems in the world is for people to turn towards the Manifestation of God, Bahá'u'lláh; to put into practice the Teachings; to see the earth as one country; and to work for the unification of all the people in the world. One very important and positive result of World War II was the creation of international systems by means of which countries could begin working together.

It is important at some time in your life to study these great letters from Shoghi Effendi.

Shoghi Effendi wrote one history book: *God Passes By*. It tells the story of the first one hundred years of the Bahá'í Faith: The ministries of the Báb, Bahá'u'lláh, and 'Abdu'l-Bahá, and the early years of the Guardianship.

This book is so important because Shoghi Effendi helps us to understand the *meaning* of the events of the early history of the Bahá'í Faith. Shoghi Effendi explains to us the correct way to view the lives and actions of the Central Figures. To prepare to write *God Passes By*, Shoghi Effendi read all the Bahá'í Writings and all works—published and unpublished—about the Faith, including all articles and books by people who were not Bahá'ís but had studied or mentioned it.

Rúhíyyih Khánum estimates he read over two hundred books. He took notes on all these which he then organised.

Rúhíyyih Khánum remembers how he worked on *God Passes By*:

How many hundreds of hours Shoghi Effendi spent on reading his sources and compiling his notes, how many days and months in painstakingly writing out in long hand—and often rewriting—the majestic procession of his chapters, how many more wearisome days he sat at his small portable typewriter, hammering away with a few fingers, sometimes ten hours on end, as he typed the final copy of his work! And how many more hours we spent late into the night, when the daily typing was over, seated side by side at his big table in his bedroom, each with three copies of the typescript before us, proof-reading, making corrections, putting in by hand the thousands of accents on transliterated words which Shogi Effendi would read aloud, until his eyes were bloodshot and blurred, his back and arms stiff with exhaustion, as we worked on to finish the entire chapter or part of the chapter he had typed that day. [92]

After he finished *God Passes By*, he wrote a history of the first one hundred years of the Faith in Persia for the Bahá'ís in Iran. Rúhíyyih Khánum could not help him with this because she did not have sufficient knowledge of the language. She could hear him chanting or reading aloud the words as he wrote, in a voice which she describes as 'infinitely plaintive.' [93]

The Guardian worked for two years on *God Passes By* while still carrying on with all his other responsibilities while in the middle of a World War, violence in the Holy Land, and being under continual attack from Covenant-breakers. Rúhíyyih Khánum remembers the suffering this brought him: 'On rare occasions it was my misfortune during these years to see him weep as if his heart would break—so great was his agony, so overwhelming the pressures that bore down upon him!' [94]

After this period and for the rest of his life—which would be thirteen more years—Shoghi Effendi wrote no more long letters or books. His communications from then on were all short notes and cables. The Bahá'í community had grown so much that anything more was not feasible. Nevertheless, he often wrote a personal note at the end of letters written by his secretaries in response to a question or news from Bahá'ís. These were often signed 'your true brother, Shoghi.'

Chapter 10

Shoghi Effendi loved architecture.

Architecture is the profession of designing buildings. It involves the art of design. After the design is finished, architects are usually involved in the construction of their work. Today architectural design is done on computers but in Shoghi Effendi's time, an architectural drawing had to be done by hand with pencil, paper, and rulers of various kinds. The drawings had to be completely accurate with every part of a building drawn according to its size with the measurements on the page. To learn to make such drawings took talent and years of training. Fortunately Shoghi Effendi had the perfect person living across the street who could help him design buildings: Sutherland Maxwell, Rúhíyyih Khánum's father. Maxwell moved to Haifa after the passing of May Maxwell and brought his vast architectural experience with him—he had won awards and was well known in his field.

Around 1942, Shoghi Effendi decided it was time to begin the design for the Shrine of the Báb. The centenary of the Declaration of the Báb was in 1944—one hundred years after the Báb declared Himself to be the Manifestation of God. The Guardian wanted to present a design to the Bahá'í World by that important date.

Sutherland Maxwell had already designed several smaller structures for him so he knew Mr Maxwell was very skilled and talented.

For Mr Maxwell, designing the Shrine of the Báb was a great privilege. He would be using all his talents and experience on a building that had great spiritual meaning and would be revered as a place of pilgrimage for centuries. So this was very satisfying for him but also a great challenge. Shoghi Effendi gave him only a few guidelines: It should blend the styles of the East and the West; it should not look like a church or a mosque; and it should have a dome on top and an 'arcade'—a covered passageway with columns.

The first drawing of the future shrine that Mr Maxwell prepared had a pyramid shaped dome which Shoghi Effendi rejected. He wanted a dome like that of Saint Peter's Cathedral in Rome, the main Cathedral of the Catholic Church, which the Guardian considered to be the most perfect dome in the world. Maxwell went back to work. The next drawing he submitted had the right proportions but was too European in style, and Shoghi Effendi asked that to be changed. Maxwell produced a third drawing with more Indian influences which Shoghi Effendi loved. The Guardian did make some changes to this one as well. He elongated the clerestory* on the second floor of the Shrine of the Báb giving the design a much more delicate look than before when it appeared too squat. The beautifully timeless design that we know today was then complete.

---

* A high section of wall with windows above eye level designed so that light comes in.

Next, Shoghi Effendi asked Maxwell to make a scale model of the Shrine which he could show to the world. It had to be ready by 23 May 1944, the centenary of the Báb's Declaration. On that afternoon, the model of the Shrine of the Báb was unveiled in the Eastern Pilgrim House in front of many Bahá'ís including some from neighbouring countries who had come to celebrate the centenary.

But the world was in the middle of a devastating war, economies of many countries were wrecked, and Bahá'ís struggled with all of this while they had been working towards the goals of the Seven-Year Plan. The beginning of the construction would have to wait another two years.

Violence broke out in Palestine after World War II. Now Shoghi Effendi had the problems of how to get the right kind of stone to the site and where to find skilled workers. So he decided to have some of the work done in Italy where there were skilled stone carvers. Hand of the Cause Ugo Giachery lived in Italy and accomplished the very difficult task of getting the stone and shipping it.

In 1948 the first excavations took place behind the site of the Shrine of the Báb to make a flat area on which the structure could be built. Shoghi Effendi was on his feet the entire day until nightfall supervising the work, even designing a small train track on which the debris could be taken away. He used all the dirt and stone that was dug up to build a terrace in front of the Shrine.

Rúhíyyih Khánum writes in a diary entry for Tuesday, 24 February 1949, that two of the cornerstones have been laid and that the construction work could now begin. Bahá'ís felt they were participating in the building of this magnificent Shrine because Shoghi Effendi wrote the Bahá'í World regularly with updates such as when large shipments of stone came in. Shoghi Effendi's messages filled them with excitement. Despite the terrible economic hardships in the world caused by the War, Bahá'ís gave sacrificially for the construction.

Rúhíyyih Khánum played a crucial role during the construction. She acted as Shoghi Effendi's representative in negotiating prices with the engineer, contractor, and importers. The Guardian was very strict about not being cheated because the funds being used had been given by Bahá'ís and because it was unjust to overcharge. So Rúhíyyih Khánum had to work hard with Shoghi Effendi refusing offers when he thought the price was not right. Once when an estimate was too high, he even threatened to stop the construction. Rúhíyyih Khánum described herself as Shoghi Effendi's 'sword' in these negotiations.

Sutherland Maxwell passed away in 1952, before the Shrine was fully finished. This gifted architect and devoted Bahá'í was able to see only part of the Shrine completed. His death was an enormous loss to Shoghi Effendi for whom he was a close friend and a kind of father figure. He shared with Maxwell a love of beauty in design. In recognition of his service, Shoghi Effendi named one of the doors of the Shrine after him, as well as one for Ugo Giachery who had worked so hard from Italy, and Leroy Ioas who had supervised much of the construction.

The Shrine of the Báb was completed in 1953. Bahá'u'lláh had chosen the site of the remains of the Báb as the centre around which the edifices of His administrative institutions would grow. Today, the

Shrine is at the heart of the Bahá'í World Centre and the seat of the Universal House of Justice is near it. Shoghi Effendi described it as the 'Queen of Carmel'.

Bahá'u'lláh revealed the Teachings of God for today. But how can they be put into practice and carried out? Individuals can read the Bahá'í Writings and try to follow them but what about groups of people from diverse backgrounds and what about entire nations? Who decides how to bring the Teachings from words on a page into our human society? How is this decided?

Without a system to carry out good ideas, good ideas remain just ideas and never become reality. People argue about whose idea is better, who has the better way of carrying out an idea, who should be in charge.

In His Writings, Bahá'u'lláh provided such a system. He gave the foundation for what became the 'Bahá'í Administrative Order'—the system which today comprises the Universal House of Justice, Spiritual Assemblies, Counsellors, and Auxiliary Board members.

'Abdu'l-Bahá sowed the seeds of the first institutions and early Bahá'í communities. He taught Bahá'ís that they must love one another. After all His travels and letters there were small groups of Bahá'í in the Near East, North America, and Europe. But they did not have a formal *system* for making decisions and carrying out plans together. They only knew that they should love one another.

Shoghi Effendi was the builder of this Administrative Order. Based on the Writings of Bahá'u'lláh and 'Abdu'l-Bahá, he established the system we have today which includes elected institutions at the local, regional, national and international levels, and individuals appointed at the local, subregional, continental, and international levels who serve in an advisory role.

One is elected by the Bahá'is (Local and National Assemblies) and the other is appointed by the Universal House of Justice (Counsellors, Auxiliary Board members).* The Assemblies have authority in their area only as a group—not as individuals. The Counsellors and Board members do not have governing authority but advise the Assemblies and individuals; guide and protect the communities; and foster learning.

The Head of the Bahá'í Administrative Order is the Universal House of Justice.

The Bahá'í institutions make decisions and determine courses of action through consultation. Consultation has as its goal the investigation of truth. It can involve sharing one's ideas, listening to those of others, and arriving at a collective decision. The Bahá'í spirit is for all Bahá'ís to support the decisions of their institutions. The purpose of the administration is to be a means by which Bahá'u'lláh's Revelation has practical impact on the world.

When Shoghi Effendi became the Guardian, many of the experienced older Bahá'ís wanted to have the Universal House of

---

* There are also regional institutions called regional Bahá'í councils and local committees such as the area teaching committees.

Justice formed immediately. But he knew that there were too few institutions and too little understanding of the Bahá'í Writings to elect the Universal House of Justice. He was also concerned that powerful individuals would try to take over the Bahá'í community if its institutions were weak.

He concentrated the efforts of Bahá'ís on founding Local and National Assemblies. These would be the foundation on which the Universal House of Justice could be built.

In 1951 he created the first international Bahá'í institution—the International Bahá'í Council—and began appointing Hands of the Cause to serve in various parts of the world. The Council would be a forerunner to the Universal House of Justice. It was not an independent consultative body—rather its role was to assist the Guardian as his representative in all affairs related to the new government of Israel (a country founded a few years earlier), and in developing the Bahá'í World Centre. The Hands of the Cause travelled internationally to encourage the teaching of the Bahá'í Faith and to protect the Bahá'í community from division.

Rúhíyyih Khánum was appointed to serve on the Council and as a Hand of the Cause, showing the great faith Shoghi Effendi had in her capacity.

The Guardian explained to Bahá'ís that the development of the administrative order was guided by three 'charters' (a written document that founds and gives rights and a mission to a country or organisation): [95]

1. Bahá'u'lláh's *Tablet of Carmel:* In this Tablet, God is 'speaking' to Mt. Carmel and says, 'Rejoice, for God hath in this Day established upon thee His throne, hath made thee the dawning-place of His signs and the dayspring of the evidences of His Revelation.' Mt. Carmel is where the holy remains of the Báb and those of 'Abdu'l-Bahá are buried and where the seat of the Universal House of Justice is located.

2. 'Abdu'l-Bahá 's *Will and Testament* which protected the unity of the Faith by appointing Shoghi Effendi as Guardian and calling for the future election and establishment of the Universal House of Justice as ordained by Bahá'u'lláh.

3. 'Abdu'l-Bahá 's *Tablets of the Divine Plan* which were the Master's call to teach the Faith throughout the world

The first charter was about Mt. Carmel as the centre of the Faith, the second charter was about safeguarding a future Administrative Order so the Faith could grow on a solid foundation, and the third charter was about taking the Bahá'í Faith to the entire world.

In 1953, Shoghi Effendi launched the Ten-Year Crusade. This was the first internationally coordinated teaching plan between multiple countries. It came after a series of national plans that the Guardian organised such as the Seven-Year Plan in which he called on American Bahá'ís to settle in each country of Latin America and the Caribbean.

Shoghi Effendi announced the Ten-Year Crusade in his Riḍván message of 1952: 'The primary aim of this Spiritual Crusade is none other than the conquest of the citadels of men's hearts. The theatre of its operations is the entire planet.'[96]

The standard bearers of this plan would be the Hands of the Cause, which included Rúhíyyih Khánum. A standard bearer is someone who carries the flag in a battle to inspire the soldiers.

The major goal of the Ten-Year Crusade was to settle Bahá'ís in all the countries of the world. Each Bahá'í who was the first to settle in a country where there were no Bahá'ís would be given the title of Knight of Bahá'u'lláh. Even today, if a new country is created and you go there to settle as the first Bahá'í, you will be a Knight of Bahá'u'lláh.

Four intercontinental conferences were held in 1953 to launch the Ten-Year Crusade. These took place in Kampala, Uganda; Chicago, United States; Stockholm, Sweden, and New Delhi, India. To each Shoghi Effendi sent a Hand of the Cause as his representative. Rúhíyyih Khánum attended the conference in Chicago as his representative.

The response of the Bahá'ís to the pioneering call was immediate. Two-hundred and fifty-four Bahá'ís went out and opened 121 countries and territories to the Faith. Shoghi Effendi kept meticulous records of each pioneer, from what country they had left, and in which they settled. Since childhood, Shoghi Effendi had always kept lists and records. He wrote by hand the names of each Knight of Bahá'u'lláh on a specially designed map which he had made.

Rúhíyyih Khánum remembers many nights when she saw Shoghi Effendi leaning over his maps, carefully studying them and adding names and details. She thought of the Guardian in those moments as the 'great mapmaker' who was leading the Bahá'í world and recording every one of its successes without any rest or thought for himself:

I remember so vividly how he worked on his own map of the goals of the Ten-Year Plan. He was tired out and run down after his long winter's work in Haifa, with the Shrine, the gardens, the pilgrims, the interminable and ever-increasing correspondence. With difficulty I had extracted a quasi-promise that when he took a cure, to a well-known watering place, he would really rest and devote himself for that period at least to his health. The pleasant summer sun was shining outside, the long leafy alleys of trees, through which one went to drink from various waters at specific times, were shady in the heat, it all beckoned to drowsy relaxation—but Shoghi Effendi spent the hours of daylight leaning over his map. Filling in its details with infinite care. All my remembrances and those of his doctor, my indignant reminder of his promise, had no effect. He was wholly absorbed in his task, forgetful of tired muscles, strained eyes, over-worked brain.[97]

Chapter 11

In November 1957, Shoghi Effendi was in London with Rúhíyyih Khánum to purchase items for the new Archives building which was being built on Mt. Carmel. The flu was going around, and Shoghi Effendi caught it. Gradually he developed a fever.

Still, he asked Rúhíyyih Khánum to have a large table put in his room on which he could spread out his maps. He was still reading reports and correspondence every day. Rúhíyyih Khánum and his regular doctor in London both advised him to rest. But he did not feel he could fall behind in the work of the great Ten-Year Crusade. The Bahá'í world was at the halfway point of the Crusade, and he wanted to make a map filled in with all the progress which had been made so far. He leaned over the table to fill one in with such care that there would be no errors.

In the early morning of 4 November, Rúhíyyih Khánum came into Shoghi Effendi's room to see how he was feeling. He was lying down in a comfortable position with his eyes slightly open.

But Shoghi Effendi was no longer there. He had left this life and gone to the Abhá Kingdom.

Bahá'ís knew that Shoghi Effendi was a human being and that all human beings die. But no one really thought about the possibility of *Shoghi Effendi* dying. Bahá'ís could not conceive of their world without him. He was their leader, their infallible guide, their friend and co-worker—and yet, when Rúhíyyih Khánum found him that morning, he was gone.

Even though the unthinkable had happened and even though the shock was overwhelming, Rúhíyyih Khánum had to do *something*. She remembered that the shock of 'Abdu'l-Bahá's passing had almost killed her own mother, May Maxwell. She wondered how many people would suffer when hearing this news out of the blue, and who would not survive it.

She decided to send three cables spaced out over two days to make the terrible blow a little easier. First she cabled the International Bahá'í Council, then some hours later, the Hands of the Cause, then the following day the National Assemblies: 'Beloved all hearts precious Guardian Cause God passed peacefully away yesterday after Asiatic flu ...'[98]

The first people to whom Rúhíyyih Khánum turned were her coworkers, the Hands of the Cause. Hasan Balyuzi, an Iranian Bahá'í who would be known for the many history books about the Faith, which he later wrote, lived in London, as did John Ferraby, an Englishman of Jewish background who served for years on the British National Spiritual Assembly. Dr Ugo Giachery, an Italian aristocrat from Sicily who had been responsible for getting all the marble for the Shrine in Haifa, was in London by that evening. Amelia Collins, an American who served on the International Bahá'í

Council and donated very generously for the building projects at the World Centre, arrived the next day.

According to the Burial Laws set forth by Bahá'u'lláh, a deceased person's body must be buried within one hour's travel time from where they pass away. This can be an hour by car, on foot, or by train, but within one hour is the general principle. The body of a deceased Bahá'í must be washed before being wrapped and buried. A body must not be cremated. It should be allowed to disintegrate naturally. Because it was the temple of the soul, a body, even when there is no life in it, must be respected and not damaged.

Rúhíyyih Khánum asked Dr Adelbert Mühlschlegel to wash Shoghi Effendi's body. He arrived from Germany with Dr Hermann Grossmann; both men had served on the National Spiritual Assembly of Germany-Austria, and suffered and served in Germany throughout the Nazi years. Dr Mühlschlegel prayed next to the body of the Guardian and carefully washed it and anointed it with attar of rose. Then it was wrapped in nine yards of white silk bought by Rúhíyyih Khánum.

Over the next days, the rest of the Hands of the Cause arrived. They met the night before the funeral to choose the devotional readings.

Shoghi Effendi was buried at the New Southgate Cemetery in London. John Ferraby wrote a description of that day:

The Great Guardian was carried in and laid on the soft green covering of the catafalque. The Chapel was crowded to the doors, and many had to remain outside. All stood while the wonderful prayer, ordained by Bahá'u'lláh for the dead, was chanted in Arabic ...

In solemn file the friends followed the casket as it was borne out, placed in the hearse again and slowly driven the few hundred yards to the graveside. There it was gently deposited at the head of the grave, so that when the beloved Guardian's remains were lowered into it he would face east to the Qiblih of the Faith ...

As all stood, silently waiting for the coffin to be lowered into the grave, Rúhíyyih Khánum felt the agony of the hearts around her penetrate into her own great grief. He was their Guardian. He was going forever from their eyes, suddenly snatched from them by the immutable decree of God ... For over two hours the believers, eastern and western, filed by. For the most part they knelt and kissed the edge or the handle of the casket ... Children bowed their little heads beside their mothers, old men wept ... The morning had been sunny and fair; now a gentle shower started and sprinkled a few drops on the coffin, as if nature herself were suddenly moved to tears. Some placed little flasks of Persian attar-of-rose at the head; one hesitatingly laid a red rose on the casket, symbol no doubt of the owner's heart; one could not bear the few drops of rain above that blessed, hidden face, and timidly wiped them off as he knelt; others with convulsed fingers carried away a little of the earth near the casket. Tears, tears and kisses, and solemn inner vows were poured out at the head

*of the one who had always called himself their 'true brother',
When the last believers in this grief-stricken procession had
filed by, Rúhíyyih Khánum approached the casket, kissed it
and knelt in prayer for a moment. She then had the green
pall spread over it, laid the blue-and-gold brocade from the
innermost Shrine of Bahá'u'lláh on top of it and arranged
the still-fragrant jasmine flowers over all its length. Then the
mortal remains of him whom 'Abdu'l-Bahá designated 'the
most wondrous, unique and priceless pearl that doth gleam
from out the Twin Surging Seas' were slowly lowered into the
vault, amid walls covered with evergreen boughs and studded
with flowers, to rest upon the rug from the Holy Tomb at Bahjí.
A prayer was then chanted in Persian, and the Afnán Hand of
the Cause, Hasan Balyuzi, read the closing prayer in English.*

*All this time—a service that had lasted almost four hours—the
representative of the Israeli Government, obviously deeply
moved, had been in attendance, himself stepping beside the
coffin and, with bowed head, paying his solemn respects. He
and the majority of the mourners now left, the Hands of the
Cause, the National Spiritual Assemblies and Auxiliary Board
members remaining behind by previous arrangement to see
the vault sealed.*

*Prayers were then said in many foreign languages and by
friends from distant countries, and the orange and olive leaves
brought from the Garden of Riḍván in Baghdád by Tarázulláh
Samandari—the only living Hand of the Cause who was*

privileged to enter the presence of Bahá'u'lláh—were placed on the grave, as well as the flowers brought by Leroy Ioas from the Bahá'í Gardens in the Holy Land ... Over the tomb, at his feet, like a shield of crimson and white, lay the fragrant sheath of blooms which had covered his casket, and heaped about was a rich carpet of exquisite flowers, symbols of the love, the suffering, of so many hearts, and no doubt the silent bearers of vows to make the Spirit of the Guardian happy now, to fulfil his plans, carry on his work, be worthy at last of the love and inspired self-sacrificing he gave them for thirty-six years of his life. [99]

After the funeral, Rúhíyyih Khánum was faced with a challenging task: To design a monument for Shoghi Effendi's grave that would match his great station. As she was leaving the burial site, the image came to her of a single white Corinthian column topped by a globe, upon which a large, golden eagle seemed to be either taking off or landing. While travelling in Edinburgh, Shoghi Effendi had purchased the statue of an eagle in this same position and had brought it back to Haifa and placed it in his bedroom, which was also his office. He had also expressed to her the desire to have his own Corinthian column, which surprised her since she didn't see how he could use just one column. This is the design of the monument that we see when we visit the gravesite today. The original model of the eagle remains in the Archives building.

Corinthian is an ancient Greek design in which the stone column is topped by a basket with acanthus leaves around it. This type of basket was used to give offerings to God. Above it is the globe, meaning the earth, and atop it is the eagle which symbolises Shoghi Effendi's majesty. In one sense, the offering to God is an earth over which the Bahá'í Teachings have been spread by Shoghi Effendi as the Guardian of the Bahá'í Faith.

We can't know how the loss of Shoghi Effendi felt for Rúhíyyih Khánum. To have shared her life with a person as extraordinary and unique in human history and then have him disappear is beyond our comprehension. She expressed her feelings in poems which she wrote after Shoghi Effendi's passing. When we feel great sadness, writing about our feelings really helps to deal with them.

Here she remembers her last moments with the body of Shoghi Effendi:

> I kissed his brow and took his hands
> So beautiful and soft to feel in mine
> They curved around my fingers, supine
> In death.
> I gazed upon his blessed face
> And never saw a beauty so sublime—
> It was my last look for all time—
> In agony and joy.

And her very last moment with the Guardian's body as she pulls the shroud over him:

'Twas my lips, dear
That kissed your icy brow,
My hands that folded
O'er your tranquil form
The silken shroud ...

Now, she and all the Bahá'í world were left behind:

So many pearls
And so many seas—
But the Pearl of Great Price
Slipped back into the sea
Leaving us desolate on the shore. [100]

All Bahá'ís were now on their own. They could only move ahead on faith that the promises of the Bahá'í teachings and their vision of the future were real. Faith is when you believe in something with conviction. But if you have faith, you can take one step forward at a time even when faced with great adversity.

Part 3

Hand of the Cause of God

Chapter 12

Faith is what the Hands of the Cause needed most. Shoghi Effendi was gone. They were, according to his writings, the 'Chief Stewards' of the Bahá'í community. A steward is someone who is responsible for an organisation or property and must protect it, care for it, and guide it.

Immediately after the funeral and filled with feelings of grief and uncertainty, Rúhíyyih Khánum and four other Hands of the Cause returned to the Holy Land. They entered Shoghi Effendi's room and sealed it with wax and taped the safe in which he kept all his important papers.

Three days later, on 18 November, they were joined by the rest of the Hands of the Cause and held a memorial for the Guardian. They were all meeting together as a group, a conclave, to consult on what to do next.

The following morning nine Hands of the Cause were appointed to go back into Shoghi Effendi's room and open the safe to look for his Will and Testament and any instructions he might have left them. But they found none.

The Bahá'í community was now in a very fragile state: there was no clear leader based on the Writings. The system that was designed by the Master and Shoghi Effendi based on Bahá'u'lláh's Writings should have a Guardian and the Universal of Justice as the Head of the Faith. But the Guardian had no children, and there was no will.

The Hands of the Cause described their feelings to the Bahá'í community:

> *The first effect of the realization that no successor to Shoghi Effendi could have been appointed by him was to plunge the Hands of the Cause into the very abyss of despair.*[101]

At this point, they remembered the complete sacrifice that Shoghi Effendi had made. He had laid the groundwork upon which to build the World Order of Bahá'u'lláh:

> *Has not the World Center, with its sacred Shrines and institutions, been firmly established? Has not the Message been established in countries and dependencies? Have not the National and Regional Spiritual Assemblies, forerunners of the Universal House of Justice, been implanted in twenty-six great areas of all continents? Has not the Guardian left us not only his incomparable translations, for English-reading Bahá'ís, of the Bahá'í Sacred Literature but also his own master works of interpretation which disclose to us the unshatterable edifice of evolving Bahá'í Order and world community? Has not the Guardian, building upon the enduring foundation of the Master's Tablets of the Divine Plan, created the World Crusade to guide our work until 1963?*[102]

Bahá'ís would focus on teaching the Faith and reaching the goals of the Ten-Year Crusade by 1963. In that year, when enough National Assemblies had come into existence, the Universal House of Justice would be elected.

Until then, the Hands of the Cause would organise themselves to guide the Bahá'í world. According to the Master's Will and Testament, there should be a body of nine Hands of the Cause in the Holy Land. The conclave of Hands appointed nine from among themselves to serve as the Custodians of the Faith until the election of the Universal House of Justice in 1963. Rúhíyyih Khánum was one of those nine. Once it was elected, the House of Justice would become the Head of the Bahá'í world. The creation of the House of Justice is called for in the Writings of Bahá'u'lláh. The worldwide Bahá'í community would then be completely safe from division, under the shelter of the Covenant.

For five years, 1958-1963, the Bahá'í World was guided by the Hands of the Cause in the spirit of Shoghi Effendi. It was like crossing a stormy ocean until the ship reached the safety of land which in this case was the election of the Universal House of Justice.

Rúhíyyih Khánum served as one of the Hands of the Cause in the Holy Land—the Custodians who helped coordinate the affairs of the Bahá'í World to win the goals of the Ten-Year Crusade.

One of her responsibilities was to attend the Intercontinental Conference in Kampala, Uganda, in 1958. Shoghi Effendi had called for the holding of such conferences in the middle of the Crusade. When Bahá'ís get together and review their accomplishments and consult on their challenges, they often become enthusiastic and motivated to serve the Cause, and they give each other encouragement.

The Kampala Conference was held in January 1958. Shoghi Effendi had wanted the Conference to take place around the same time as the laying of the cornerstone of the House of Worship, the Mother Temple of Africa—it was the first one that would be built on that continent. The Arabic term for 'House of Worship' in the Bahá'í Writings is *Mashriqu'l-Adhkár*, meaning 'dawning-place of the mention of God'. They are nine-sided and people of all faiths are welcome to visit and pray. In the future each one will have a hospital, orphanage, dispensary, and school built around it. The Hands of the Cause predicted that the House of Worship in Kampala would be 'a mighty silent teacher of the Faith.' [103]

Shoghi Effendi explained that these Houses of Worship should be places where people go and pray and have their spirits lifted so that they will then go out and serve others. Otherwise, the Houses of Worship will be full of beautiful words but won't be of any help to society. That is why such buildings as schools will be near the Houses of Worship in the future.

Over nine hundred Bahá'ís attended the Kampala Conference from as far away as Japan. Rúhíyyih Khánum brought the photograph of Bahá'u'lláh from the World Centre. Bahá'ís are not allowed to use this photograph in their homes or events because of the holiness of the Manifestation of God. Bahá'ís also do not draw pictures or paintings of Bahá'u'lláh for the same reason.

After prayers were offered, the attendees walked past the photograph with reverence and in silence. Then Rúhíyyih Khánum anointed each with attar of rose which was used on special occasions by 'Abdu'l-Bahá.

She brought other gifts as well. There was a silver box with earth from Bahá'u'lláh's Shrine and a piece of the plaster from the prison of Mahku, the isolated prison where the Báb had revealed the Bayán., His Holy Book. These were placed beneath the building's foundation. With these sacred objects in it, the Temple would be symbolically connected to the Holy Land.

The goals for the next five years for Africa were reviewed using large maps and many people volunteered to pioneer and contributed money for the growth of the Faith in Africa. If a Bahá'í cannot go pioneering because they have other obligations that they can't ignore, they can offer funds to support someone else to go.

Rúhíyyih Khánum spoke about the qualities of Shoghi Effendi. Hearing about the Guardian from someone who had been with him every day as his wife and helper inspired the audience and increased their dedication. She remembered that she felt a great power come from him:

Everybody who had the great privilege of knowing the Guardian recognized in him tremendous power; he not only had great spiritual and mental power which radiated from him, he had an electric something in his nature which was like being in the presence of a very powerful dynamo. I have been in electric plants where dynamos have generated electrical power for a whole city; the whole building shook and vibrated with the force that was being created in those generators. I have witnessed, myself, for twenty years, the strange force which emanated from Shoghi Effendi. This emanation from the Guardian was so strong that when he was not in the house, I felt less of it; when he was up on the mountain in the gardens of the Shrine, I would feel the force of it diminish; when he was in Bahji, I would feel still less of it; and if we were not in the same city, I would not feel it. It was a very extraordinary thing, and it was not my imagination. [104]

She spoke of his humility:

The one characteristic of that heart was the most extraordinary and true humility I have ever seen. He had, of course, like any other human being, self-respect. But he had no pride whatsoever—no pride in his own person, no pride in his station; but when it came to this religion, then he had a fiery pride. He would never tolerate any insult or any slight that reflected on him as Guardian, nor on the Faith of Bahá'u'lláh. But in his own nature he was the quintessence of humility. [105]

Being humble is a sign of great inner strength. When people brag and boast about themselves, they often feel weak inside and need to be noticed by others. Humility makes you free of that. Nothing can hurt your feelings when your ego is not involved. Rúhíyyih Khánum helped the participants feel the humble love that Shoghi Effendi had for them. He had high hopes for the growth of the Faith in Africa.

Three years later, in January 1961, Rúhíyyih Khánum participated in the dedication of the completed Mother Temple of Africa. The House of Worship was in Kampala at the top of Kikaya Hill, Kampala, Uganda. Shoghi Effendi and Hand of the Cause Mason Remey conceived of its design which blended in perfectly with the scenery around it. With its soft green dome, sand-coloured rough-finished walls, the temple appears to emerge naturally out of the land itself. From the inside, you look up at a blue dome and around at soft green walls. While you are inside and praying the temple feels like an expression of nature and, ultimately, of God, the Creator.

Shoghi Effendi had decided that a House of Worship should be built in Uganda because of the many Bahá'í activities that had developed in East Africa and all the teaching that was taking place. He had set aside a beautiful Persian carpet for the temple which Rúhíyyih Khánum then brought with her. She had it hung above the door that faced the Shrine of Bahá'u'lláh. The Shrine is the Qiblih, which means 'direction' in Arabic and signifies where we should face when saying the obligatory prayer. The Shrine of Bahá'u'lláh is the 'Point of Adoration'.

On the morning of the dedication, Bahá'ís walked up the hill. Flowers blossomed in red, orange, yellow, and purple, under a cloudless January sky. They made their way through the nine gardens that radiated from each of the nine doors of the temple. They stepped inside onto beautiful Persian carpets which had been given by Iranian Bahá'ís.

Rúhíyyih Khánum was the first to speak that morning. She brought the spirit of the Guardian with her and praised the African believers. Then prayers were read in many languages including several African ones: Ateso (Uganda/Kenya), Luganda (Great Lakes Region, east Africa), Swahili (eastern and southern Africa), Lubukusu (Kenya), and Acholi (Sudan/Uganda). The next day, more than 1,500 people came for the public opening of the temple. The Bahá'ís in Uganda had invited many dignitaries and published excerpts from the Bahá'í Writings in the newspapers to prepare for this day.

Later that same year, in September of 1961, Rúhíyyih Khánum dedicated another of the completed continental Houses of Worship. This one was for Australia and located outside of Sydney.

When Rúhíyyih Khánum arrived there, the Mayor of Sydney gave her an official reception. Before the actual dedication, she and other Hands of the Cause met with Bahá'ís to talk about the teaching goals of the Ten-Year Crusade. These included teaching the Maori people of New Zealand, the native peoples of those islands. The Bahá'í Faith gives great importance to the Indigenous cultures in the world, including the islands of the Pacific. Among those attending the opening was Fred Murray, the first Australian Aboriginal Bahá'í. He lived a life of great hardship but was open to all people and respected by Bahá'ís and Aboriginal Australians. While she was in Australia, he showed Rúhíyyih Khánum how to throw a boomerang.

The House of Worship in Australia is high on a hill near the ocean. It stands on nine sets of steps that lead to the nine doors. The colour of the Temple appears white but can seem to slightly change colour depending on the sun and sky. The walls have crushed quartz in them, which is a hard, crystalline mineral. Because of its crystal quality, the walls looks like they're sparkling when there is a bright sun.

Earth from the Shrine of Bahá'u'lláh and plaster from the room in which the Báb was held prisoner at Mahku had been placed in the foundation of the Temple in 1958. For the opening dedication, Rúhíyyih Khánum brought a magnificent green silk carpet which Shoghi Effendi had set aside for the Temple and had it hung on the door that opened in the direction of the Qiblih.

Rúhíyyih Khánum greeted the Bahá'ís who had come from many different places, including large islands in the South Pacific such as Tahiti and dedicated the new Temple in honour of Shoghi Effendi.

On 21 April 1963, in the house of 'Abdu'l-Bahá—where Shoghi Effendi had also lived—the Universal House of Justice was born. This institution had been promised in Bahá'u'lláh's *Tablet of Carmel*, one of the Charters of the New World Order.

Bahá'u'lláh explained that:

It is incumbent upon the Trustees of the House of Justice to take counsel together regarding those things which have not outwardly been revealed in the Book, and to enforce that which is agreeable to them. God will verily inspire them with whatsoever He willeth, and He, verily, is the Provider, the Omniscient.[106]

One role of the Universal House of Justice is to apply the Bahá'í Teachings to issues that come up in the future. The world is always changing. New inventions come into being, new discoveries are made. New opportunities and challenges will appear that we can't even imagine today. The Universal House of Justice consults the Writings, as well as experts and experienced Bahá'ís and applies the Bahá'í Teachings to new situations. It can bring new laws into existence but not cannot change those revealed by Bahá'u'lláh.

The Universal House of Justice is the Centre of Bahá'u'lláh's Covenant, as were 'Abdu'l-Bahá and the Guardian. The Guardian and the Universal House of Justice are the 'twin successors' of 'Abdu'l-Bahá. Bahá'ís look to the Universal House of Justice for guidance on how to develop Bahá'í communities in the light of the Teachings in an ever-changing world. Bahá'ís follow and obey the Universal House of Justice and work in a spirit of cooperation and consultation with each other and their institutions. This preserves the unity of the Bahá'í world and, in the future, the unity of the entire world. 'Abdu'l-Bahá wrote that the 'Universal House of Justice, likewise, wardeth off all differences and whatever it prescribeth must be accepted.'[107]

The Universal House of Justice will be a refuge for the world of the future like the ark was in the time of Noah when the people who got in it were saved from the flood. Shoghi Effendi described the Universal House of Justice as 'the exponent and guardian of that Divine Justice which can alone insure the security of, and establish the reign of law and order in, a strangely disordered world.'[108]

The election of the Universal House of Justice in 1963 was a turning point in world history, like the appointment of 'Abdu'l-Bahá as the Centre of the Covenant and Shoghi Effendi as the Guardian. The Bahá'í World and its future were in a secure place, protected from attack from the outside and division from within by the Covenant now embodied by the Universal House of Justice.

On 21 April 1963, the first ever International Bahá'í Convention for the Election of the Universal House of Justice began, one-hundred years after the first Riḍván when Bahá'u'lláh declared to His Followers that He was the Manifestation of God. Rúhíyyih Khánum greeted the delegates. They were seated in the main area of the house of 'Abdu'l-Bahá. She gave the instructions, two prayers were read, and in absolute quiet the delegates filled out their ballots.

Rúhíyyih Khánum then called out the names of countries in alphabetical order. The delegates from each country came forward in order and placed their ballot in a special box. All of this happened in complete silence and with a profound sense of dignity. Everyone in the room knew that they were witnessing an event of immense historical significance—after it, there would be no turning back. Hand of the Cause Paul Haney remembers:

When the balloting was completed every one felt that Bahá'u'lláh had indeed been present in that gathering and that a unique and wonderful pattern had been established for the world to marvel at and, in the fullness of time, to follow.[109]

Eighteen tellers from a variety of countries went to count the ballots. The delegates gathered to have sessions during which they consulted about the affairs of the Bahá'í World. During their free time they could go and pray at the Shrine of the Báb.

The next day, 22 April, Rúhíyyih Khánum announced the results of the election. The nine elected members of the Universal House of Justice came up to receive the love of the delegates and to be greeted by Rúhíyyih Khánum.

The Universal House of Justice, the Supreme governing body of the Bahá'í World had been born in a quiet, dignified, and simple election.

The Hands of the Cause then signed a document stating that they relinquished control and authority over the Bahá'í community, and these now rested with the Universal House of Justice alone. A unique event in world religious history had just taken place!

Chapter 13

Bahá'u'lláh declared that He was the Manifestation of God in 1863 in the Garden of Riḍván near Baghdád. The year 1963 marked the 100th anniversary of this most important of events. The Bahá'í World planned to hold a celebration in Baghdad but the situation for Bahá'ís there was too dangerous so it was held in London where the Bahá'ís could visit the grave of the Guardian which was near that city.

The year 1963 was also the end of the Ten-Year Crusade launched by Shoghi Effendi during which Bahá'ís had gone to pioneer all over the world. So this First Bahá'í World Congress was both a celebration of the Declaration of Bahá'u'lláh and of the achievements of the Ten-Year Crusade.

The teaching efforts of Bahá'ís brought the Faith to many new parts of the world, so the First World Congress showed the increasing diversity of the Bahá'í community. There were people from many diverse cultures.

The Bahá'ís at the First World Congress also witnessed one of the promises of Bahá'u'lláh come true: The Universal House of Justice members were presented to the Bahá'í world for the first time. The Bahá'í Faith had survived the Covenant-breaking during the time of 'Abdu'l-Bahá and Shoghi Effendi and the unexpected loss of the

Guardian. Yet it had made it through with the help of the Hands of the Cause and, after the period of the Custodians, the Universal House Justice was brought into existence.

Rúhíyyih Khánum opened and closed the Congress which went from Sunday 28 April to Thursday 2 May. She spoke of the many blessings of Bahá'u'lláh that had helped the Bahá'í World achieve the goals of the Ten-Year Crusade. Now they must look to the future. Bahá'u'lláh '... has promised that He will always help those who arise to serve him ...' and serving is '... the way we show our love for Bahá'u'lláh, our love for Abdu'l-Bahá ... our love for the Guardian, who wore himself out and burned himself up in leading the way and showing us how we could go forward ...'[110]

There were many distinguished Bahá'ís, and everyone could be inspired by their stories and the love they expressed. Among them were Amoz Gibson and Tarázu'lláh Samandarí. Gibson was the first African-American to serve on the Universal House of Justice. His father, William, had become a Bahá'í shortly after the visit of 'Abdu'l-Bahá to Washington DC in 1912. Gibson and his wife, Mary, travelled extensively to teach the Bahá'í Faith. They settled on the Navajo Reservation in Arizona and, inspired by them, other Bahá'ís moved there to introduce the Faith to the Native people.

Tarázu'lláh Samandarí was a Hand of the Cause from Iran who had met Bahá'u'lláh three times during his youth in 'Akká in 1891–2. Born in Iran, his grandmother had been a companion of Táhirih, one of the Letters of the Living. He became an accomplished calligrapher and copied by hand many of the Bahá'í Writings—this was long before the Xerox machine.

Mr Samandari met Bahá'u'lláh when he went with family members overland from Iran to 'Akká for pilgrimage. He stayed six months in 'Akká and was received into the Presence of Bahá'u'lláh three times, once in the House of 'Abbúd in 'Akká, another time at the Mansion of Bahjí in the countryside and one other time. On two occasions, Hand of the Cause Samandari witnessed Bahá'u'lláh revealing the Bahá'í Writings. He also was present at two of the most momentous events in Bahá'í history: the reading of Bahá'u'lláh's Will and Testament, the *Book of the Covenant* (the *Kitáb-i-'Ahd*) and the first election of the Universal House of Justice.

On the third day of the Congress the members of the newly elected Universal House of Justice were presented: Charles Wolcott, Ali Nakhjavani, Borrah Kavelin, Ian Semple, Lutfu'llah Hakim, David Hofman, Hugh Chance, Amoz Gibson, and Hushmand Fatheazam. The first ever letter announcing a plan from the Universal of Justice was then read aloud by David Hofman, who had been a professional actor and so had a wonderful reading voice. The first plan was the Nine-Year Plan which was to last from 1964 to 1973.

Rúhíyyih Khánum was the final speaker of the First Bahá'í World Congress. She remembered Shoghi Effendi, her beloved who had so recently passed away. She described his beautiful eyes and his complete humility: 'He hadn't one speck of personal pride or conceit in his entire make-up; but when it came to the Cause of God, he was a lion ... nothing could interfere with what he considered right.'

During his entire life as the Guardian, he could never rest: 'So much of his life was suffering ... he was deeply sensitive and loving and he was ground down all his life through the actions and words of others ...'. She ended her talk with a plea to the Bahá'ís gathered there and throughout the world:

Friends, do not fail Shoghi Effendi. You have not finished with him and he has not finished with you. It is the time to put your step on new trails. To make new vows ... to go out and please Shoghi Effendi and make him happier than he ever was in this world ... Let us carry on the work of our beloved Lord, Bahá'u'lláh, every day of our lives, because we are His people and we are blessed far beyond our deserts. [111]

One of the main themes spoken about at the Congress was teaching of the Bahá'í Faith to the masses of humanity. 'Abdu'l-Bahá used the term 'entry by troops', a troop being large group of people. Each Bahá'í is called on by Bahá'u'lláh to teach the Bahá'í Faith. This is because the Bahá'í Faith is the Religion of God for this day, and only if the message is shared can people learn about it and benefit from its spiritual forces. The Bahá'í Faith is not a closed private club; it is for everyone and open to all. When we teach, we are giving the gift of spiritual knowledge.

During the late 1950s and 1960s, people in India and parts of Africa became Bahá'ís in large numbers. When people become

Bahá'ís they must be educated ('deepened' is the word Bahá'ís use for this) in the Bahá'í teachings. The recognition of Bahá'u'lláh by large numbers of people presented Bahá'í communities with a big educational challenge!*

One of the countries in which the Bahá'ís were engaged in mass teaching was India, a country which has one of the largest populations in the world, much of it living in the countryside. Some time after the World Congress, Rúhíyyih Khánum decided to make a trip throughout India to encourage the Bahá'ís and participate in the mass teaching. One of her duties as a Hand of the Cause was to encourage the teaching of the Bahá'í Faith around the world.

This major trip was the first of many that she would make now that she no longer had to remain in the Holy Land.

Rúhíyyih Khánum's constant companion for the rest of her life was Violette Nakhjavani, who was the daughter of Samiheh Ardestani and Hand of the Cause Musa Banani. Mr Banani was a Bahá'í from Iran of Jewish background. Mr and Mrs Banani pioneered to Uganda. Among his many services, Mr Banani secured the land for the House of Worship that was later built in Kampala, Uganda. Violette Nakhjavani also pioneered to Uganda with her husband, Ali Nakhjavani. She then devoted herself to assisting Rúhíyyih Khánum after the Guardian passed away.

The trip to India began in February 1964. These months brought exhilarating experiences for Rúhíyyih Khánum as she experienced

---

* Later, the Ruhi Institute would be developed to address this challenge.

new cultures and met enthusiastic, devoted Bahá'ís. About teaching on this trip, Rúhíyyih Khánum later wrote:

It is my firm conviction that whatever good such a visit may have done, whatever effect it may have produced on the community of Bahá'u'lláh in that part of the world, the one who derived the greatest instruction from it was myself. I am the one who received most, who was most changed by it, the one most blessed by the privilege of meeting so many wonderful fellow believers. Truly, in seeking to teach this glorious Faith of Bahá'u'lláh the teacher is taught. [112]

India is a huge country. There are hundreds of millions of people from many different religions, including Hindus, Buddhists, Jains, and Muslims. There are twenty-two official languages, 122 major languages, and over 1,500 local and regional languages. When Rúhíyyih Khánum and Violette Nakhjavani landed in India, they had no idea of the size, the joy, and the difficulties of the journey they were undertaking.

This teaching trip took them through thirteen of the sixteen states of India, to over seventy villages, many of which were remote. They travelled almost 88,000 kilometers† by plane, car, boat, and Jeep, and on foot, and visited the neighbouring countries of Sri Lanka, Nepal, Thailand, and Sikkim during the peak of the sweltering summer!

---

† 55,000 miles

The trip brought great joy as well as hardships. Rúhíyyih Khánum suffered with the intense heat, the distances, and the exhausting schedule of constantly meeting people. There were constant demands on her. She was there to encourage so she did her best to hide the ill health from which she often suffered.

Putting a garland of flowers around someone's neck is a gesture of hospitality in India. Bahá'ís were so honoured to have Rúhíyyih Khánum come to India that when she came off the plane, twenty-two garlands were put around her neck! Despite the long trip, she met with Bahá'ís that evening, and the following day she went to the plot of land on which the future House of Worship for India was going to be built. The name of the old village that had been on that land happened to be 'Baha-pur'—the 'Settlement of Baha'.

The next stop for Rúhíyyih Khánum was the 'pink city' of Jaipur, called that because of the general colour of its buildings—soft dark pink. It was the largest city in the largest state of India, Rajasthan, famous for its many historic castles.

To meet the Bahá'ís in Jaipur, she put on for the first time a beautiful old Rajasthani tie-dye silk-satin sari which she had brought from Haifa with her. The sari is the traditional dress for women of all South Asia. It consists of a single piece of cloth that is wrapped around the waist then draped over the shoulder under which there are undergarments. She told the Indian Bahá'ís that when she wore a sari she felt like a true Indian lady. From this moment, she wore saris for the rest of the seven-month trip. Putting on a sari correctly is quite difficult if one is not used to it. Thankfully, Shirin Bowman, was there to help show her how to do it.

Ms Bowman was of Zoroastrian background and among the first Bahá'ís to be actively involved in mass teaching in India. By the end of the 1950s, there were about 1,000 Bahá'ís in India. In 1960, Bowman visited several times the remote village of Kweitiopani in Central India. A tribal people called the Bhils lived there who had ancient roots in the area. After three weeks she invited anyone in the village who believed what they had heard about Bahá'u'lláh to sign declaration cards. Seventy-five per cent of the village of 200 people signed—though most gave their thumb-prints because they were illiterate.

Because of the success of this and other efforts, the National Spiritual Assembly of India bought a Jeep for Ms Bowman, and she and other teachers continued to teach throughout the countryside. These efforts multiplied and grew. By the time of Rúhíyyih Khánum's visit in 1964, there were almost one hundred thousand new Bahá'ís in India and ten years later, there were almost four-hundred thousand!

The first village Rúhíyyih Khánum* visited was Nayala, located near the city of Agra, famous for the Taj Mahal. This white marble mausoleum is famous for its beauty. Though it is a mausoleum—a monument meant to house the burial chamber of a deceased person— the beauty of the Taj Mahal makes it look like a love poem from the king who built it, to the queen who is buried inside. 'Abdu'l-Bahá

---

* Whenever Rúhíyyih Khánum is mentioned in this account, that includes Violette Nakhjavani and other travelling companions.

once said that this magnificent expression of love in stone could one day inspire designs of Bahá'í Houses of Worship.

To get to the village of Nayala required driving over rough dusty terrain. Rúhíyyih Khánum finally reached the entrance of the village which had a colourful gateway decorated with saris, paper cuttings, and fresh flowers. Brightly coloured rickshaws were all around, having brought guests to meet Rúhíyyih Khánum. A rickshaw is a chair pulled by a bicycle, and is used in many places as an easy mode of transportation.

A wedding was happening. This was one of the seasons of the year in India when it was considered good luck to get married, so everywhere Rúhíyyih Khánum went for these first weeks, there were weddings. The family was honoured to have Rúhíyyih Khánum there. About a thousand people gathered around to hear her. She sat on a chair on an embankment outside the bride's father's house. Gradually many ladies came out but they kept their faces hidden.

This was the first time that Rúhíyyih Khánum had ever spoken to a large group of farmers and their families. After Shirin Bowman introduced the Faith to the audience, Rúhíyyih Khánum began by telling everyone of the high position Bahá'u'lláh gave to the farmer who was the one who provided food for the world.

A person is a good public speaker when they express ideas in a way that connects to an audience. Rúhíyyih Khánum showed here that she was able to do just that. She wanted to explain the relationship between the Bahá'í Faith and the religions of the past. She looked around and saw an ox-cart, a common vehicle used in villages. She pointed to the wheel of the cart and said:

The strength of the wheel lies in the hub. The wheel will be strong to the degree to which each spoke is fitted evenly and carefully into the hub. The spokes must all be the same length, all equal, and the rim must be strong, but the strength of the wheel lies in the hub. We might say that the rim of the wheel is like humanity, all of us; the spokes of the wheel are like the different nations and religions, all equal; the hub of the wheel is the Bahá'í Faith, what Bahá'u'lláh, the Founder of this Faith, has brought to the world today. Everything He teaches is to produce unity and brotherhood; into His system the nations and religions of the world can fit as equals, each finding its place, thus uniting the spokes and the rim to make the wheel; and with the provision of this Hub, the wheel can turn and pull the load forward, and so we will progress into the future, into the new kind of world that lies before us, and towards the fulfilment of mankind's great destiny.[113]

After her talk, the father of the bridegroom stood up and told the audience that he was a Bahá'í and would answer any of their questions and that they were welcome to stay longer in the village if they wanted. He then offered Rúhíyyih Khánum eleven rupees for the teaching fund. He expressed his deep gratitude for having had such a distinguished guest at his son's wedding. He then introduced his son, the bridegroom, who was just sixteen years old and shy.

Rúhíyyih Khánum and her companions were then invited into the house where the women had gathered—men and women often celebrated separately, especially in villages where people were more traditional. The young bride was seated on a stool in the middle of the room. Her head, neck, and wrists were covered in gold ornaments and she had a gold brocade sari on. She kept her face hidden from her guests. The young girls all around her were also dressed in their best and brightest clothes. They circled around her and encouraged her to remove her veil, which she did gradually. Soon a shy friendly smile came across her face.

Next, they travelled to Madhya Pradesh where much mass teaching had taken place especially in the region of the town of Gwalior which included 500 villages where almost 20,000 Bahá'ís lived. Travelling in the region was difficult because there were bandits on the road so Rúhíyyih Khánum could not travel after dark. In each village she visited, a conference for Bahá'ís was organised. In the village of Baghchini, 2,000 people were in attendance.

In the model village of Nat Kapura, the inhabitants were the Nath people. They were snake catchers and charmers. Snake charmers went way back in Indian history and may have originally been healers. The snake was considered holy in traditional Hinduism so these charmers may have been calling on the power of gods to heal snake bites and other afflictions. Rúhíyyih Khánum spoke to the villagers there, she again used an image they could understand. She praised a young man who had danced on a pole with a dangerous snake around his neck while he played the flute. Then she said there was an even more dangerous snake in life—that of hatred and jealousy.

Rúhíyyih Khánum also visited very poor villages lived in by people considered 'untouchable'. Over centuries, India developed a caste system in which people belonged to groups which were higher or lower to each other. The Brahmins were the highest caste. The untouchables were the lowest, and they were shunned by all people. No one would associate with them. Among the Bahá'ís, these villagers saw greater equality. The Bahá'í teachers in the school who came among them were of the Brahmin caste. The fact that the Bahá'í Faith had no caste system had great appeal to many Hindus of lower caste.

In one of the untouchable villages, the only Bahá'í man there came up shyly after the meeting to give Rúhíyyih Khánum a gift of the images of three Hindu Gods and a small silver incense burner. She was moved by this kind and spontaneous gesture and asked later what gift she could give the Bahá'ís there. She was told that several Bahá'í schools had no light so she bought and distributed a pressure lamp to each school in the area that had no light.

Rúhíyyih Khánum's last public event in Madya Pradesh was to dedicate a new building in the town of Gwalior as a teaching institute. Shirin Bowman lived there so it was a centre of mass teaching. These institutes were necessary to help educate people in the Bahá'í Faith so they could, in turn, educate the many new believers.

Several hundred Bahá'ís came from neighbouring villages and stood along the road leading to the new institute building. The hall was decorated with colourful paper cuttings and balloons. There were large paintings on the wall illustrating the major principles of the Bahá'í Faith. Rúhíyyih Khánum cut the blue ribbon which officially opened the institute. There was a great deal of excitement in the audience and many speeches and prayers were given in Hindi, one of the official languages of India. In her talk, Rúhíyyih Khánum described the life and suffering of Bahá'u'lláh and reminded everyone that our words must be adorned with good action.

One of the people who gave an enthusiastic talk that day, was a man who served as the keeper of the temple in his village. He was of the Brahmin caste—the highest one. He had been up all-night speaking with a Bahá'í teacher about the Faith and now, here he was with Indians from all castes proclaiming the greatness of the Bahá'í teachings.

Shoghi Effendi, 1919.

Rúhíyyih Khánum, circa 1950s.

Rúhíyyih Khánum, circa 1960s.

Rúhíyyih Khánum with Fred Murray.
Bahá'í World Conference, 1963.

Start of African tour with Violette Nakhjavani.
Uganda, December 1969.

Rúhíyyih Khánum with His Highness the Asantehene, Otumfuo Opoku Ware II
of the Asante. Kumasi, Ghana, September 1971.

Rúhíyyih Khánum visiting Gbendembou village.
Sierra Leon, September 1971.

Rúhíyyih Khánum with Fujita.
October 1971.

Rúhíyyih Khánum visiting Mokuni.
Southern Zambia, circa 1970s.

Chapter 14

India is a country with several ancient religions each with many different branches. The major religions of India are Hinduism, Islám, Buddhism, and Jainism. There are also areas of India which have Christians and now, Bahá'ís, as well as people with animistic beliefs— that is the belief that objects, places, and creatures all possess a distinct spiritual essence.

Hinduism is by far the most widespread religion in India. The exact origins of Hinduism are unknown. The *Vedas* and the *Upanishads* are the main holy writings for Hindus. Their exact origins are also unknown because they are so ancient. They include a wide variety of spiritual literature on subjects such as the soul, the Divine World, the history of Hinduism, and the gods as they act in the world. Some texts are considered to have been revealed by the Divine and some are texts that are remembered and written down by people. Originally in the Sanskrit language, they were meant to be recited aloud and are written as poetry.

Rúhíyyih Khánum and Violette Nakhjavani drove 700 miles with the assistance of Shirin Bowman's daughter who spoke the local languages and could help them find the way to their next destination, the region of Ujjain. This city is on a hot plateau in Central India and is one of the seven centres of pilgrimage for Hindus. Because of this, there are many large temples dedicated to different gods.

On their way to this great city, the travellers stopped in the city of Sanchi to see one of the oldest stone structures in India, the Great Stupa at Sanchi. A stupa is a building, usually round and tower-like, that contain a holy relic, which has objects in it connected with a Buddhist holy person. Buddhism began in what is today Eastern India with the life of Siddhartha Gautama, the Buddha. He was born a prince and lived in a palace until he experienced spiritual enlightenment. The term 'Buddha' means the 'enlightened One.' He understood the nature of life and that people had to become completely detached from the world to be free of suffering. He lived sometime between the 6th and 4th centuries before Jesus Christ. There are many Buddhist holy writings but their exact origins are not known. They have been passed down for hundreds of generations and have contributed a lot to the spiritual understanding of millions of people. Buddhism spread from India into Tibet, China, the rest of East Asia, and Central Asia.

At Sanchi, Rúhíyyih Khánum and her companions saw a peasant coming up the hill towards the stupa in the middle of the noon day heat with a small child in his arms and two other children walking next to him. Rúhíyyih Khánum asked him why he had come to this place. He said he was a field labourer from another part of the state and heard this was a holy place. He wanted to bring his children and pay his respects and receive a blessing. He was Hindu and a poor man but his actions showed Rúhíyyih Khánum that Indians had a sense of spirituality.

Rúhíyyih Khánum next visited Kwetiapani, the first Bahá'í village in India, home of the Bhil people and located in a dusty dry area. In honour of Rúhíyyih Khánum's visit all the oxen of the village had their horns painted green, read, and blue. She was given the Hindu blessing of 'arti' in which a chosen lady brings a polished brass tray which might have rice grains, sweets, coconuts, a lighted candle, incense water, and sandalwood paste or red powder with which a mark is made on the forehead of the guest of honour. She was then invited to sit in a cart which was then pulled to the local Bahá'í Centre. Villagers dressed in green with bells on, amd danced to the sounds of flutes and drums as the cart moved forward.

The next day, Rúhíyyih Khánum went to the town of Shajapur even though she had a fever. She was met by a brass band, garlands, and flowers, and men shooting their rifles in the air as a way of welcoming her. In this town, she ate her first Indian meal in the traditional style. Food was served on metal trays that were put on the carpet on the floor. But there were no knives or forks. So Rúhíyyih Khánum whispered to another guest to please begin eating. This way she could see how it was done with their hands and bread. Then she followed the example.

On the drive back to the city of Ujjain the next day, the travellers stopped in the home of Mr Dayaram Malvia in the village of Harsodan. Hand of the Cause Dorothy Baker had visited the village in 1953.

Ms Baker met 'Abdu'l-Bahá in 1912 and travelled extensively in the United States and the rest of the Americas to teach the Faith. Later, as a Hand of the Cause, she travelled internationally to India and other countries before being killed in a plane crash. It was in the home of Mr Malvia that plans were made for teaching the masses in the area about the Bahá'í Faith.

The Festival of Holi was being celebrated in the village. This is an ancient Hindu festival celebrating the arrival of spring in all its colours. During these five days, there are no castes in India. There are bonfires every night and people throw coloured powder on each other. This was the one time when Rúhíyyih Khánum had free time to go out and see the famous temples in Ujjain. After she had been out for the morning, she returned covered in all kinds of coloured powders and laughing.

Even though this demanding schedule made her quite tired and sick, she never wanted to let the Bahá'ís down. When she heard that she had been expected in a small village, she insisted on going there despite the approach of night. By the time she arrived, the villagers had dispersed, having given up seeing her. Then word got around that she had come. Villagers quickly came from all over and gathered around her. In the darkness her presence was a light. It uplifted their spirits.

The main hub of teaching activities was the nearby city of Indore, the largest city in Madhya Pradesh, the state in which most of the Bahá'ís of India lived. The first teaching institute founded in India was located there. A Bahá'í teacher lived permanently at the institute.

Selected students from all over came to study the Bahá'í Writings and learned to be effective teachers. As a result of this kind of education, new Bahá'ís who were too shy to speak of the Faith became confident teachers.

Rúhíyyih Khánum met with the teachers from the area, encouraging them never to become discouraged, to love all people, and to be assured of Bahá'u'lláh's Guidance in all their spiritual efforts. She spoke to them of two great teachers of the Faith whom she had known: Martha Root and her mother, May. Root used to say: 'Step aside and let Bahá'u'lláh do it.' This means that when we want to teach the Faith we must try to present it with a pure heart and without involving our own egos, to teach for the love of God.

On 8 March, Rúhíyyih Khánum landed in Bombay, a major city on the India Ocean. It is where the Faith was first established in India, going back to the time of the Báb.

Despite having a fever, she went to a reception in her honour at a hotel where 300 people showed up to meet and listen to her. Newspaper reporters and photographers were there to cover the whole event as well as members of Bombay society from all professions—educators, political leaders, and businessmen. Rúhíyyih Khánum got up to speak. Her fever rose to a temperature of 38 degrees Celsius. Still she spoke. She encouraged her audience to look to their great spiritual heritage and take their part in the unfolding destiny of humankind.

---

*   102 degrees Fahrenheit

The next day, she had tea with the governor of Maharashtra, the state of which Bombay was the capital. Though her fever continued into the evening, she did not want to disappoint Bahá'ís who had gathered to hear her in a local hall. She started to speak, but fifteen minutes into her talk, she needed to leave. Before she got out of the hall, she fainted.

Rúhíyyih Khánum badly needed to rest and recover from all her exertions. At the same time, a large conference had been planned in an area where people were eager to hear about the Bahá'í Faith. She did not want to disappoint them and yet she could not attend as her body was too weak.

So she asked her companion Violette Nakhjavani to go in her place. Ms Nakhjavani protested that all the Bahá'ís wanted to see Rúhíyyih Khánum and not her. But Rúhíyyih Khánum insisted. She had great confidence that Ms Nakhjavani and Ms Bowman could convey important spiritual messages to the Bahá'ís and connect them to the spirit of the Bahá'í World Centre in the Holy Land.

Having to do this caused Ms Nakhjavani intense distress but she did it anyway. She knew that it was very important for them to encourage the Bahá'ís in their efforts. Rúhíyyih Khánum explained to her that different types of speakers appealed to different people. One person gets up and speaks, and she can reach certain people. Then, if another person gets up to speak, she may reach people who had not understood or listened before. This helped Ms Nakhjavani see that she and Ms Bowman had an important part to play.

After a week, Rúhíyyih Khánum was feeling well again. She travelled to the village of Mohal, twenty-five miles out of Bombay. Five hundred people came out to see and hear her. The headman of the village introduced Rúhíyyih Khánum and told the audience to learn about the Bahá'í Teachings. Then Rúhíyyih Khánum told them stories to show the purpose of the Faith in the world.

Many people were interested in the Faith in this area because of the teaching efforts of an elderly believer who worked as a baker. This humble man always began his talks on the Faith this way: 'I only speak a broken Hindi, a few words of English, and a very poor Persian. Combining all these languages, and adding to them the language of Love, I have come to tell you about a great Message and a Divine Messenger—Bahá'u'lláh.' This direct and humble way of teaching was very effective. Several thousand people in the area had become Bahá'ís through him.

In her next talks in Bombay and the city of Poona, the second largest city in Maharashtra, she gave Bahá'ís a personal glimpse of Shoghi Effendi:

You know, the beloved Guardian Shoghi Effendi had beautiful, beautiful eyes. They were sometimes hazel coloured and sometimes very grey, and they changed in the light, and some people thought they were blue, which they were not. These eyes, when he got excited about something, about the work of the Cause, he would open so wide that they looked like two suns rising above the horizon. The thing that brought him the greatest happiness, during the twenty years that I had the privilege of serving him, was news of the expansion of the Cause of God. You know of his sufferings and of the disloyalty and the enmity of his own family. The only thing that consoled him was this news of the opening of new countries, new territories, new Local Spiritual Assemblies, and the increase in the number of believers.[114]

Rúhíyyih Khánum then headed south to the large and beautiful city of Bangalore—the capital of the state of Karnataka—because there was a great deal of enthusiasm for the Faith in that region. In the village of Karampalyo, she visited the home of a devoted Bahá'í pioneer family. The sound of drums was heard, meaning that it was time to attend a ceremony for the laying of the foundation stone for the new Bahá'í Centre in the village. Many villagers awaited her. She was given the blessing of 'arti'. Because she was much taller than most Indian women, she humbly bent forward so the lady could reach her forehead.

For the next five days, she visited villages in the area. There was much teaching going on, and she laid two more cornerstones for Bahá'í centres. Then she was asked to open a new village. It was the custom among Bahá'ís in the area to invite travelling Bahá'í teachers to open a village which meant to go there and be the first to tell them about the coming of Bahá'u'lláh.

Rúhíyyih Khánum was invited to open the village of Kadagrahara, 'Jungle Village', which was two miles from where they had laid the second cornerstone. But it grew dark, and there was no sign of the Jeep. Rúhíyyih Khánum was nervous that people in her village would go to sleep, and she would miss her chance. She decided that she and the others would walk the two miles. She was wearing a simple sari common to village women.

She felt intimidated about opening a village as she had never done this before. But she had been asked to do it by the local Bahá'ís, and one of the main Bahá'í teachers in this area told her that this was her village to open, so she went. The whole experience made a great impression on her so she wrote about it later:

We arrived in the dark village to the sound of furiously barking dogs. Here and there a candle-lighted doorway showed the people in their humble homes. A mud-plastered, stone house, the whitewash peeling off and leaving soft reddish mottling on the cream-coloured walls, had a door flanked by two huge stone slabs, like refectory tables, and at the ends of these were two tall thin slabs standing upright. I was told to sit on this bench, and curled up, cross-legged, against the wall. Our kerosene pressure lamp was hung up on one of the stone poles. Before us were two immense palm trees framing the clear, almost full moon. Gradually the villagers gathered, bringing clean straw mats for people to sit on, men, women and children, mothers with babies in their arms. It was a village of what used to be 'untouchables', labourers of the lowest caste. One must remember that this kind of teaching is entirely new to me. I told them that I had heard in India that the sacred water of the Ganges is carried away to be shared by all who desire to drink of it, that in this spirit we had come to them to share the message of this day, and so on. They listened intently; one man's face held my eyes as he concentrated on every word. After me others spoke, including the son of the Headman of another village in which I had laid the cornerstone. He is a truly beautiful boy, getting his Master's degree in physics, though his father is almost illiterate. A fellow student, taking the same degree and also a Bahá'í, was with us. The village-teacher (meaning the National Assembly appointed teacher for this area) also spoke. His fine dark face and chiseled features, his grey hair, the gestures of his long, sensitive hands were a sight to watch in the moonlight. He lacked all his front teeth. But the dignity, a certain selflessness, the deep conviction, the wonderful oratorical powers of these people are so great that blemishes are scarcely noted. Analyzing what happened, it amounts to this: we told them that all religions expect the Promised One, quoting Krishna particularly (the Hindu Bahá'í teacher did this); gave them a brief history of the Faith, pointed out the needs and dangers of the world today; gave them the principles and more of the teachings (we must have spoken an hour and a half); told them something of the Faith abroad; demonstrated the answer it holds for the future of a peaceful, united world; and asked them if they did not wish to become Bahá'ís. Twenty-one, including two women, said they did. I found that the man who had listened so intently was their Headman; he also became a Bahá'í ... [115]

Rúhíyyih Khánum was astonished by this reaction. Where she grew up in Canada, the US, and Europe, it took a very long time for even one person to become a Bahá'í. She realised now that people anywhere in the world could recognise the truth and accept it immediately if they were ready.

Next, after a difficult and tiring ride, Rúhíyyih Khánum arrived in the village of Matakere. Over a thousand people were there to meet her. Her hosts placed plastic chairs under the branches of a tree to protect her from the sun. The audience sat on the ground in front of her. While she spoke, the women and children stitched together large leaves using small bamboo splinters. The men had long thick hair and wore big earrings. The representative of the regional government was there. Six young girls came up shyly to recite Bahá'í prayers they had been taught the day before by a Bahá'í teacher.

Rúhíyyih Khánum spoke to them about Bahá'u'lláh and His Life and the great love He had for all people, especially pure-hearted people such as them. Hearing this caused great excitement among the villagers. An elderly man with long grey matted hair stood up and said that first the government had come to help them with material things such as buildings and schools and now this beloved mother had come to bring them a message of true love which we should accept without hesitation. Many of the villagers accepted the Faith.

The villagers were organised into different clans according to the work they did. There were the honey-gatherers, the basket-weavers, and the woodcutters. Each group had its own rules. Watching all of this were several Indians from the state of Rajasthan who had settled in the area but did not want to mix in with the villagers whom they looked down on.

When the speaking part was finished, a group of men came up to perform a local traditional dance. Then the villagers who lived far away left, because they had ten miles to walk to get home.

Rúhíyyih Khánum sat cross-legged on the ground with the other women and ate boiled rice and lentil sauce which was placed in the large leaves. The leaves were so well sewn together that nothing leaked or fell out of them. There were women who wanted their names inscribed as Bahá'ís and others, even friends, who did not. Rúhíyyih Khánum marvelled at how independent the women were in making up their own minds.

The road back was difficult but Rúhíyyih Khánum was happy because of what she had just experienced. Ms Nakhjavani remembered how much 'Abdu'l-Bahá had longed to travel everywhere, even if on foot, to teach the Faith but could not, and here was the wife of his grandson doing just that.

Chapter 15

Rúhíyyih Khánum flew to the port city of Cochin on the south-western Indian coast in the State of Kerala, known for its beautiful beaches, mountains, and many canals. Near Cochin there were about sixteen islands. Bahá'ís lived on most of these. Rúhíyyih Khánum took a two-and a half-hour ferry ride to the island of Nayar Ambalam. The beautiful ride over the waves under a blue sky and the site of tree covered islands brought joy to the travellers to the point where they started singing aloud!

Over a thousand islanders were waiting for Rúhíyyih Khánum around the local schoolhouse. As she approached, local girls formed two rows. They cast petals onto the ground in front of her so that she would walk on a carpet of flowers.

The headman of the high school on a nearby island introduced her. He apologised that he did not know anything about the Bahá'í Faith and thought he had been asked because he could speak English well. Rúhíyyih Khánum's talk so moved him that he wanted to be accepted that day as a Bahá'í. More than fifty other islanders expressed their desire to be Bahá'ís.

Children then performed comedy skits for the guests. People stayed until almost midnight. A local fisherman and his wife invited

Rúhíyyih Khánum to stay with them. They gave their guests their bed and best linen for the night and slept elsewhere.

From 20 April to 7 May 1964, Rúhíyyih Khánum left India to attend several Bahá'í National Conventions in nearby countries before returning to complete her teaching trip. It was customary in those days for Hands of the Cause to personally visit Bahá'í National Conventions to deliver the Message from the Universal House of Justice and to encourage and inspire Bahá'ís with their presence.

Rúhíyyih Khánum flew to the capital of the island of Ceylon, today renamed Sri Lanka. This large island is an independent nation—the first nation to have a female Prime Minister—located in the Indian Ocean just off the southern tip of India. It is famous for its great natural beauty and its wide variety of animals—including elephants, leopards, and crocodiles. The oldest known tree in the world, a fig tree, is in Sri Lanka.

Sri Lanka has lush green countryside. While walking through the forest to get to a village, Rúhíyyih Khánum got leeches on her. These worms live in fresh water and can attach themselves to skin. Then they suck a person's blood. Their bodies grow bigger until they have had enough and fall off. She had to get them off because they leave scars that itch a lot. To get them off, Rúhíyyih Khánum poured salt on them. This made them lose their grip and fall off. Leeches are fascinating creatures and, Rúhíyyih Khánum, who loved animals, was thrilled to see them after hearing so much about them as a child.

After three days in Sri Lanka during which she attended the Convention and met with Bahá'ís in the countryside, she left for Kuala Lumpur, in the nation of Malaysia. In that year of 1964, the Malaysian Bahá'í community was electing its first National Spiritual Assembly. There was great joy over this because Malaysia had different ethnic groups—Malay, Chinese, Filipino, Indigenous peoples—and these did not always get along. The two major groups, Malay and Chinese, were also of different religions, Islam and Buddhism. The convention showed that unity between these groups was possible, that they could unite under the banner of the Bahá'í Faith.

Bangkok, Thailand, was Rúhíyyih Khánum's next stop. After her arrival, she spoke at a large banquet with many diplomats in attendance. Then she went to the Israeli Ambassador's residence but soon after, she fell ill. She was unable to attend the opening of the Bahá'í Convention. Fortunately, Hand of the Cause Dr Muhajir was there and could deliver the message from the Universal House of Justice.

Dr Muhajir had been an active teacher of the Faith since he was a child in Iran. Right after high school he pioneered to the northern Iranian province of Azerbaijan for two years and began many local Bahá'í activities there. He trained as a doctor and, at the beginning of the Ten-Year Crusade, decided with his wife Iran, to pioneer to the Mentawai Islands which are in the Indian Ocean. Miraculously, Dr Muhajir was assigned by the Indonesian government as a doctor to these very islands! He was the first modern doctor there. He worked together with the traditional healers whom the people had used for centuries. He even put on the traditional makeup of the local healers so people would feel more comfortable around him and understand that he was a healer. After being appointed a Hand of the Cause, he travelled the world constantly teaching the Faith and encouraging others to do the same.

Rúhíyyih Khánum's last two stops on this trip were the Himalayan Kingdoms of Nepal and Sikkim. The Himalayan Mountains are the world's youngest and tallest mountains. They form an arc over northern India. This tall range blocks the rain clouds from going north so India has a very wet rainy season called the monsoon.

The Bahá'í Faith first arrived in Nepal around 1952. Contact with local Bahá'ís had been lost but with the help of Bahá'ís in the neighbouring country of Sikkim, Rúhíyyih Khánum met them. She encouraged them in their teaching. The community, comprised of mostly young well-educated men who knew a great deal about the Faith, was enthusiastic about this visit and was especially happy to know that raising a National Assembly in Nepal was one of the goals of the new Nine-Year Plan.

To get to their last destination, the mountain kingdom of Sikkim, Rúhíyyih Khánum had to go down the mountains into the Indian plains where the city of Calcutta was located. From there, they drove back up into the mountains towards the capital of Sikkim, the small city of Gangtok. The road went up and up into the tall mountains and constantly curved. There were almost no straight sections of road. Early in the trip, the Jeep broke down. Rúhíyyih Khánum and her companions were put into the front cab of a large truck that was going to Sikkim. The eight-ton truck was hauling eighty-five live sheep.

Sikkim dates to the 1600s when a Buddhist Kingdom was founded. Though small, there are eleven official languages spoken there and two main religions—Buddhism and Hinduism. It has some of the tallest mountains in the world and thrilling, majestic scenery. The people of Tibet, which borders it, are closely related to the Sikkimese.

Kedarnath Pradham, a Bahá'í of Nepalese background whose ancestors lived in Sikkim for a long time, was the main Bahá'í teacher. Rúhíyyih Khánum found that many of the local Bahá'ís were capable women who were outspoken, courageous, and independent. Many became Bahá'ís without their husbands. The chairperson of the Local Assembly of Gangtok was a young and confident woman.

Rúhíyyih Khánum had an audience with the King and Queen of the Sikkim. Mr Pradham advised Rúhíyyih Khánum that it was a sign of respect in Sikkim to present someone with a white scarf called a 'khada'. So she bought two of these and presented them to the King and Queen. The King expressed his appreciation for them and then immediately returned the scarves to them. Doing this was a sign of respect on the part of the two royals.

Rúhíyyih Khánum answered their questions about the Faith. The Queen was a young American woman, Hope Cooke. She met the King while on a student visit to India, and they later married. She heard of the Faith back in the United States. Mr Pradham had also given them books on the Faith on a previous visit which she had read.

That same day, Rúhíyyih Khánum set out for the village of Pakyong, a small village where Mr Pradham lived and which was a centre of Bahá'í activities. The drive was only twelve miles but over very rough roads—some very steep and muddy and others strewn with boulders—and narrow suspension bridges which had to be driven over extremely slowly.

It was well worth it. Many people from neighbouring villages awaited Rúhíyyih Khánum with garlands of flowers and white scarves all of which they placed around her neck. She spoke to them with great love.

At night, as she slept, she could hear people speaking in the house. Visitors from other villages stayed up all night asking questions of the Bahá'í teachers.

The next day was a Bahá'í Holy Day, the anniversary of the Declaration of the Báb. People began coming to the house as early as seven in the morning. The first group to arrive was from an all-Bahá'í village, Panche Basty. Men from there had invited Rúhíyyih Khánum the day before to visit their village where they had built a school and hired a teacher. They were told, though, that there was not time in the schedule to undertake the mountainous journey.

The women of Panche Basty were not satisfied with that answer and came over to see Rúhíyyih Khánum themselves. For three hours, they presented arguments as to why she should come. Rúhíyyih Khánum knew it was impossible, so she told them she would visit on her next trip to which they answered that many of the elder people would have passed on by then! Rúhíyyih Khánum invited them instead to all come there that day but they said they had built beautiful arches in her honour which they couldn't bring. She explained that she was not well enough to climb those mountains and return on the same day. The women offered with absolute sincerity to carry her to the village while she could sleep in their arms. Finally Rúhíyyih Khánum was able to prevail and sent a boy to the village to invite everyone to come to the house.

Over the course of the Holy Day, there was much music, dancing, and songs sung by the ladies. Rúhíyyih Khánum gave several talks in which she told the villagers of her dreams of the Faith as a girl that then caused her to accept it immediately.

In the afternoon, Rúhíyyih Khánum accompanied barefoot the women of Panche Basty halfway up the mountain. They parted amid tears and Rúhíyyih Khánum sang a melody for 'Alláh'u'Abhá' which she had learned in Africa, and which they sang back with her, the sounds of their voices echoing in the mountains.

Rúhíyyih Khánum caught an intestinal bug in Bombay that continued to make her sick. When she returned to Calcutta from Sikkim, she did not feel well at all and often had to stay in bed. In one village, she felt so ill that all she could eat were four saltine crackers. Despite this, she persisted in her teaching efforts, meeting with officials, giving talks, and going to villages.

She travelled next to the state of Orissa on the Eastern coast of India. There had not been as much Bahá'í teaching activity in this state so Rúhíyyih Khánum spent two weeks there travelling the countryside and cities.

In the village of Barhana, a young man asked Rúhíyyih Khánum a challenging question about why he should accept a new religion when they had ancient ones of their own. She answered that all religions teach us how to become better, more spiritual people. Today, though, the followers of religions of the past do not agree with one another and never will. The Bahá'í Faith is a new world religion under which all people can unite. The different peoples around the world are then no longer constrained by the traditions of the past. It is the *fulfilment of all religions* so the essential spiritual teachings of the past are contained within it. It is the *eternal Religion of God* that is being revealed again for this new day. By accepting the Bahá'í Faith, a person does not give up their religion, but rather their conception of religion now embraces all of God's messengers throughout history.

From Orissa, Rúhíyyih Khánum was determined to go to the Bastar District of the state of Chhattisgarh, which is known for its lush forests, waterfalls, and temples. The state of Chhattisgarh is inland on the western side of Orissa. She wanted to go there because there were tribal people living in the forest several of whom had become Bahá'ís.

The mud roads into the forest were barely passable because the monsoon rains had begun. The monsoon season is when the main winds change direction and bring a season of intense rain. So much rain falls that people stay indoors and wait for it to pass. These rains go on for a whole season.

Many tigers lived in the forest so the villagers hired a hunter from the outside to come and kill one that had eaten 126 people.

Few people came to the meeting in a village three miles inside the jungle. Rúhíyyih Khánum was told that this was because the night before there had been the first major rain so everyone celebrated. Then the men went to hunt especially for rats which were large and plentiful and could provide them with a great deal of meat. The villagers still used bows and arrows to hunt rather than guns.

These people were very far removed from the rest of India so Rúhíyyih Khánum was not sure how to explain the Faith to them. She did this by relating it to their current situation. Here is the conversation between Rúhíyyih Khánum and the forest dwellers:

'You know they are building a road from the town to your village?'

'Yes.'

'Do you like the road?'

'Yes.'

'You know the road is bringing that great world outside here to you; when you go among the people of the town do you feel at a disadvantage, inferior to them?'

'Yes, we are afraid of them too.'

'Well, there is nothing unusual in that; all people are afraid of something ... We are all afraid of things that are different from what we are used to, but feeling at a disadvantage and inferior is something else. This is why we have come to tell you about Bahá'u'lláh, because if each one of you is a Bahá'í, and understands what Bahá'u'lláh teaches, you will not only be equal to the people of the city but superior to them. I will give you an example of what I mean. Say one of you is a Bahá'í and he goes to the city and begins to talk to a city man. He says, 'Where are you from?' And you say, 'Bastar', and he looks at you with contempt because you are an uneducated tribal man from the jungle. You say, 'I am sorry I do not speak your language; what we need is an extra language we can all learn so all the people of the world can speak to each other direct and understand each other.' The city man looks at you and is very surprised to hear such words. He says, 'Where did you get such an idea?' And you say, 'I am a Bahá'í and my religion teaches that all men are brothers and this is the day when we must all work together to bring peace to the world. We believe all the peoples and nations are equal, that all religions are from the same root, that men and women are equal, like the two wings of a bird.' The city man cannot believe his ears! He says to himself, '... his ideas are more advanced than mine; he is more tolerant than we are and his mind broader than ours.' Then he becomes friendly and asks you questions and you can tell him the wonderful teachings of Bahá'u'lláh.'[116]

This exchange pleased these people of the forest who smiled warmly while speaking with Rúhíyyih Khánum.

The week spent in the forests of Bastar were among the most joyful for Rúhíyyih Khánum.

The time had come for her to leave India for a while. Her duty as a Hand of the Cause was calling her back to Europe where she would now go to dedicate the new House of Worship in Germany.

Chapter 16

When she was a young woman, Rúhíyyih Khánum spent much time serving the Bahá'í community in Germany. By 1964 the community of Germany had successfully completed building a House of Worship. Rúhíyyih Khánum was asked to go to the opening on behalf of the Universal House of Justice. She used this opportunity to get some much-needed rest from her constant travels in India. She was familiar with Germany, and her body was adjusted to its weather and food which was important for her to feel physically better. Different climates affect people in different ways.

The Bahá'í community of Germany was persecuted when the Nazi Party came to power. In 1939 members of the National Spiritual Assembly of the Bahá'ís of Germany were arrested. Attacks against the community increased. In May 1944, seven German Bahá'ís were put on trial, and the Bahá'í 'sect' was forbidden. Bahá'ís could only do their community activities in private.

After World War II ended in 1945, the German Bahá'ís rebuilt their community. Shoghi Effendi announced that a Bahá'í House of Worship would be erected in Europe as one of the goals of the Ten-Year Crusade. He chose the site outside the village of Lagenheim in southern Germany because it was centrally located for the rest of the European countries. The House of Worship in Frankfurt is the Mother Temple of the European Continent.

Architect Teuto Rocholl's design was chosen for the Temple. It is unique among the Bahá'í Houses of Worship because it has a skeleton of exposed steel concrete on the outside instead of stone or wood. The walls are made of glass.

The Bahá'ís faced many challenges in getting the Temple built. It took years to find a good site. The Catholic and Protestant churches raised opposition to having the House of Worship of a little-known religion in Germany which was a Christian country, and many government permits had to be obtained. Finally, a location was found on a hill in the Taunus hills overlooking a scenic region of the Rhein Main region.

The opening of the House of Worship took place on 4 July 1964. Rúhíyyih Khánum spoke, and then everyone stood while she offered a prayer by Bahá'u'lláh. Then people filed by the photo of Bahá'u'lláh and the portrait of the Báb, which were both unveiled. Rúhíyyih Khánum anointed each visitor with attar of rose.

Soon, after a little rest and recuperation, Rúhíyyih Khánum returned to Ceylon (now Sri Lanka).

The three weeks she spent on this beautiful green island full of lush forests, hills, and tea plantations created great enthusiasm among the Bahá'ís there. She told them the stories of the mass teaching she had seen and experienced in India and encouraged them to do the same.

In a talk she gave to factory workers, she recounted a dream of one of the early Bahá'ís. This Bahá'í had seen in her dream a great flood drowning helpless people. Frightened, she went looking for 'Abdu'l-Bahá. He was on a hill leaning over a machine he was working on. She called out to Him to come and save all the people. He calmly explained that He was building a machine that would make the flood waters go down. Rúhíyyih Khánum interpreted this dream to mean that Bahá'ís must focus on the building of the World Order of Bahá'u'lláh which help to bring about the unity of humankind and solve many of the world's big problems.

From the capital, Colombo, Rúhíyyih Khánum travelled into the hills of central Ceylon to the ancient capital of Kandy. There, she watched with fascination the Festival of the Tooth. In ancient times, it was believed that a tooth from the Buddha's body had been saved after His cremation. In this part of the world, it is tradition to cremate a body after death. This tooth was a religious relic believed to have special powers because it had belonged to the Buddha.

A magnificent cultural festival grew up in Kandy around this relic. Rúhíyyih Khánum was eager to see it. Every year, the relic was taken out of the temple on a large elephant and a procession of elephants, lights, fire-dancers, and music would go through town and end up by the river. This colourful festival is unique to Ceylon. Rúhíyyih Khánum appreciated beauty so she must have been thrilled to see this. No matter what culture we grow up in, we can always enjoy and learn from other cultures.

In those days, most of the Bahá'ís in Ceylon were labourers who worked on the tea and rubber plantations. They had been brought from the lower castes of India by the British who had ruled India and Ceylon. While they were not educated, they were often responsive to the Bahá'í teachings when they heard about them. To speak with them, Bahá'ís had to get permission from the owners of the plantations who were happy to allow this because they had a positive impression of the Faith and knew it didn't involve politics. Strong Bahá'í communities developed in the countryside among these labourers.

Rúhíyyih Khánum told the National Spiritual Assembly of Ceylon that she was especially eager to meet the 'low caste' Ceylonese, specifically the Veddas and the Rodiyas, as she believed this is what Shoghi Effendi would have wanted her to do.

The Veddas are the original inhabitants of the island—they may have come there over 35,000 years earlier. They had always been forest dwellers and newer arrivals on the island had looked down on them as being less developed. Now their forests were getting smaller so they were losing their language and culture. They were anxious about their future.

Rúhíyyih Khánum spoke to them most lovingly and respectfully. Unfortunately, she did not speak their language. She had to use a translator, but the translator was often more interested in speaking with her than in translating her words for the audience.

At the end of her talk, the village head, who was an elderly man pointed to the camera we had. He asked that they take a photo of all of them together because it would survive long after they had passed on. This showed to Rúhíyyih Khánum that they were aware of the disappearance of their way of life.

Rúhíyyih Khánum next travelled to meet the Rodiyas, another low-caste group, in the village of Wadorassa. They were shunned by others. They weren't even allowed into villages of other Indian castes. The Rodiyas received Rúhíyyih Khánum with great warmth, performing dances and music for her. She showered them with love and spoke encouragingly to them. The Indian Bahá'ís were moved by this reception and promised to return often.

For centuries, Ceylon was the home of Theravada Buddhism. This is the oldest existing school of Buddhism going back over two-thousand years. From Ceylon, it spread to India and other parts of Asia. Its centre was the city of Anuradhapura in northern Ceylon; Rúhíyyih Khánum went to see it after her visit with the Rodiyas. At one time tens of thousands of Buddhist monks lived and studied in this city. In 288 BC, seeds from the holy Bodhi tree were planted there, making it the oldest known tree in the world whose planting date is known.

The original holy Bodhi tree is in India. One day while sitting under it, the Buddha was 'enlightened'—he understood the true nature of life: attachment to the material life caused all suffering. He began teaching people to strive for a spiritual way of life and become detached from the material world—especially from our egos. This idea is found in all world religions because it is one of the most fundamental teachings of God.

Rúhíyyih Khánum returned to India by boat. She was especially happy because her cousin, Jeanne Chute, who lived in Ceylon, was now travelling with her and Violette Nakhjavani.

They had a few free days so they visited several Hindu holy sites in that part of Southern India. A major temple dedicated to the god Shiva is in the city of Rameswaram on the Indian coast. Shiva is one of the three gods which make up the Supreme Deity in Hinduism; in traditional Christianity, God is also represented as three——God, the Father; God, the Son (Jesus); and the God the Holy Spirit.

The Bahá'í Faith teaches that there is one God—one unknowable Essence—who makes Himself known through Manifestations. Human beings know God only through His Manifestations and not directly because God is transcendent—beyond us, this world, time, and space. In older religions, such as Hinduism, God is expressed through many 'gods' who each manifest divine qualities. Shiva is the 'Destroyer' meaning he destroys the universe so that it can be re-created, destroying evil and everything that gets in the way of spiritual re-birth.

The three travellers were impressed by the intricate stone carvings on the exterior of the temples. Though they were travelling without a guide or interpreter, they appreciated how willingly local Indians engaged with them in conversations about spiritual ideas.

In the village of Trunallar, they met an exceptional Bahá'í woman who founded an orphanage. She was born in Singapore, but when she arrived in the region of Karikal in southern India, she saw how poor the people were and decided to stay and help them. She started an orphanage for young girls. Rúhíyyih Khánum spoke encouragingly to them and praised the work of this selfless woman.

In the small village of Subrayapuram, Rúhíyyih Khánum sat on the porch of an old and dilapidated temple and spoke to people of the Life of Bahá'u'lláh. Telling stories of Bahá'u'lláh's life and suffering is an excellent way of explaining the Bahá'í Teachings. After hearing Rúhíyyih Khánum speak, the local Bahá'ís in the very poor village of Terkuvalipep, decided to pool what money they had to build a small local Bahá'í Centre.

That same day, Rúhíyyih Khánum was asked to open a new village to the Bahá'í Faith, Araya Trapu, a fishing village. When she arrived at the local school to speak, there were 300 people waiting for her. People had walked for miles through rice paddies to let others know of the special unknown visitor. They also pooled their money to buy a garland of flowers to honour Rúhíyyih Khánum, though many did not even have enough food to eat. The headman of the village said that they liked what they heard about the Bahá'í Teachings and wanted to learn more. Later, if they still agreed with what they heard, they would become Bahá'ís.

In the city of Pondy, the governor of the state was eager to help Bahá'ís. He had heard of Rúhíyyih Khánum's visit to his area and gave a grand reception in her honour with many of the members of the newly elected regional Parliament. He offered to give assistance to any Bahá'í pioneer who'd settle in his region.

～

Benares is located on the Ganges River. It is the world's oldest continuously inhabited city. For centuries it was a cultural centre of India and a place of pilgrimage for Hindus. They believe that the Ganges River is holy and if one dies and is cremated along the river, the soul will escape the cycle of birth, death, and rebirth—reincarnation.

The Bahá'í Faith teaches that when we die, our souls continue to progress through all the worlds of God that are beyond this world. Reincarnation is the belief that our soul continues to be reborn into the world. Not until it is perfected can it be released from the world of suffering and attain Nirvana. The cause of suffering is our desire for the things of this world.

Only change is permanent in this material world so there is no use in becoming attached. To achieve spiritual peace, Nirvana, we must detach ourselves from the world. This difficult teaching is repeated often in the Bahá'í Writings as well.

'Abdu'l-Bahá explains that reincarnation into this world does not happen to a soul. Compared to the worlds of God, this world is imperfect. We cannot attain spiritual freedom by going through an imperfect world again and again. We must do our best in this life to grow spiritually and find inner freedom and peace—Nirvana.

The Maharaja of Benares* invited Rúhíyyih Khánum to his palace for tea and to participate in his annual festival. He was a devoted Hindu and asked questions about the Faith. Then it was time for

---

* The title 'maharaja' means 'king' but by this time, maharajas no longer had power though they were respected by the local people and lived in their old palaces on their lands.

him to go to the festival. He welcomed Rúhíyyih Khánum and her companions to watch it as well.

He walked out into his courtyard which was full of people who were going to the festival where a traditional play based on an old Indian epic was being put on. Rúhíyyih Khánum and other guests were given seats on the top of elephants from which they had an excellent view. Men covered in ash were all around the elephants. These men often wandered the countryside living outdoors and eating nothing but the food villagers offered to them. Indians considered them holy because they had rejected the world.

This is a form of asceticism which is the religious practice of denying your body any pleasures or comfort and often isolating yourself from society. While it involves a lot of discipline—which is a good thing spiritually—asceticism is not part of the Bahá'í spiritual life. We must be detached from the world but we must also be involved in the life of society to serve others.

From Benares, Rúhíyyih Khánum was driven in a Jeep to other towns. The heat was intense, and dust was everywhere. Gradually she developed a fever. She became quite ill and frail but continued to meet and speak with people and travelled several hundred miles. She cut the ribbon at the opening ceremony for the first Bahá'í Centre in the area of the city of Malhausi where 600 people waited to hear her speak and next laid the foundation stone for another Bahá'í Centre, this time in the town of Tirwa.

Finally overcome with fever, she had to stay in bed for a few days. Her cousin had to fill in for her and speak with a large audience of low-caste Indians, and then to an audience of educated medical students, and then to a group of over a thousand villagers in Ranjit Purwa. After three days her cousin was completely exhausted. Rúhíyyih Khánum had been going at this pace for months!

Rúhíyyih Khánum's great teaching trip through the Indian subcontinent ended back on Gwalior where it had started eight months earlier. Bahá'ís from all over India gathered there for an all-India Teaching Conference and one last chance to express their love for Rúhíyyih Khánum because 'They could feel that she felt herself one of them.'[117]

Rúhíyyih Khánum had fallen in love with India, its people, its many cultures, languages, and colours. Before leaving, she described the big picture of the Faith of Bahá'u'lláh:

We Bahá'ís are taught by Bahá'u'lláh that in this world there is a process which is taking place—something which had a beginning and which has an end. Bahá'u'lláh said that thousands and thousands of years ago, long before Krishna came into the world, long before Rama came into the world, long before Buddha came into the world, we had already Prophets Who came to educate human beings. He tells us that all knowledge comes from these great Divine Prophets Who come to this world to illumine the souls and the minds of human beings. He said that He has come at the top of a cycle that began thousands of years ago and His Revelation will have a direct effect on the world for 500,000 years.[118]

Chapter 17

When Rúhíyyih Khánum was in Uganda to dedicate the Mother Temple of Africa, she promised the Bahá'ís there that she would return. Nine years later she fulfilled this promise.

Rúhíyyih Khánum and Violette Nakhjavani landed in the airport at Kampala on 5 August 1970. They planned to travel across the continent by land visiting as many Bahá'í centres as possible. A large Land Rover—a vehicle that could be driven off paved roads—was purchased that was tough enough to go over the roughest terrain. The Land Rover weighed over three tons when it was fully packed with all the provisions they'd need for the journey. This would allow her to visit Bahá'ís who lived in villages and rarely saw outsiders from so far away.

Ahead of them lay four major teaching trips throughout the African continent covering thousands of miles. Over several years, she would visit many villages, give hundreds of interviews, have meetings with leaders of countries, and speak to thousands of local Bahá'ís.

They drove from Kampala to the beautiful coast lined with coconut trees and were treated to the delicious local foods often cooked in coconut juice. They came to the village of Ms Abhá, whose chief, an elderly man named Jacobi Kabwere Wonje, was licensed by the government to remove spells placed on people by witch-doctors—men and women in traditional societies who have the knowledge and power to heal and place or remove spells.

Chief Wonje was a Bahá'í. Raised in the traditional religious beliefs of his tribe, he had seventy wives and many children—in many cultures a large family is a sign of prosperity. Everyone gathered to hear Rúhíyyih Khánum and was moved by what they heard. Chief Wonje asked that a Bahá'í teacher be sent to the village to educate them further.

Rúhíyyih Khánum arrived in Dar Es Salaam in the neighbouring country of Tanzania in early September. This city grew from being a fishing village on the coast of the Indian Ocean to one of Africa's major cities. Rúhíyyih Khánum spoke at the recently opened new national Bahá'í centre about an important Bahá'í principle: Unity in diversity. The human world is diverse with many cultures, languages, and countries, and the Bahá'í Faith's mission is to unify people so that this diversity is not the cause of division but the cause of the appreciation and enjoyment of our differences.

One of the highlights of this Africa trip for Rúhíyyih Khánum was meeting the Masai people who live a traditional way of life following their herds to grazing lands. A Masai man's wealth is measured in the number of cows he owns and the number of children he has fathered. Compared to most people in the world, the Masai are quite tall. They are also known for their elaborate jewellery.

To reach the Masai area in Tanzania, Rúhíyyih Khánum had to drive roads that had become very muddy because of the heavy rains.

She drove the Land Rover herself, and it required a lot of arm strength to keep the heavy vehicle going straight. Her shoulders hurt for days after. But she insisted on going because she promised the Bahá'ís she would visit them. She was moved to meet an elderly Masai man who was serving on the Bahá'í area teaching committee and working to teach others about the Faith.

The next country on the Africa trip was Ethiopia where Rúhíyyih Khánum and Violette Nakhjavani spent a month. Ethiopia is an ancient Kingdom that was among the first to adopt Christianity as its official religion. Back in the 4th century it was called Aksum. Ethiopians are Coptic Christians, a form of Christianity which came down from Egypt. Their beliefs are like other traditional Christians like the Catholic Church but their rituals are very different.

In the capital, Addis Ababa, Rúhíyyih Khánum was given an audience with Emperor Haile Selassie, the ruler of Ethiopia. When the guests entered the room they bowed before the king. He motioned for them to sit down. Usually people were not allowed to sit in his presence but he made an exception for important foreigners like Rúhíyyih Khánum.

When they were all seated, Haile Selassie told her to 'proceed.' This disconcerted her because she had not come like an ordinary petitioner to ask for something. But she had to say *something*! So she spoke about how much she admired him and all the things he was doing for his country. Haile Selassie was making significant efforts to modernise Ethiopia. He seemed moved by her sincerity and continued the conversation despite all the petitioners waiting in the outside room to see him.

Haile Selassie asked her how many Bahá'ís there were in Ethiopia. She answered that there were 'some, Your Majesty, under the protection of your Majesty's wing.' She explained that Bahá'ís would be his most loyal citizens as obedience to government was a Bahá'í teaching. Explaining this to the king showed Rúhíyyih Khánum's wisdom because all kings fear that their subjects will revolt against them. Her comments must have assured him. He stated that in his country people were free to practice whichever religion they chose.

When Haile Selassie asked about the Bahá'í Faith itself, Rúhíyyih Khánum explained that religion was always unfolding over time, that the human race was maturing, that all Revelations come from God, and that the Messenger of the new Revelation for this day was Bahá'u'lláh.

Before leaving, Rúhíyyih Khánum presented Haile Selassie with a handmade silver box from Iran, a country whose craftsmen are known for their high-quality work. He accepted it with gratitude and, in turn, gave his visitors a gold medal commemorating his coronation.

Rúhíyyih Khánum next drove to the Gemeto region where the first ever Ethiopian Bahá'í Conference was going to be held. The head of the region insisted that she be accompanied by the governor of the area and the chief of police. This was a sign of his respect for the guests.

The conference was held under a large tent borrowed from the army. Women from Addis Ababa prepared meals in large pots. There was much joy and fellowship.

Rúhíyyih Khánum laid foundation stones for a village school, a teaching institute, and a local Bahá'í Centre. These were going to be built on two pieces of land donated by local Bahá'ís.

Village youth performed a rarely seen dance for their visitors and sang songs in English Persian, and Amharic—the official language of Ethiopia. They had learned the songs recently and despite not speaking Persian or English, the youth pronounced every word clearly.

The conference was crowned with the celebration of the Birth of the Báb. An elderly man rose and said to Rúhíyyih Khánum that 'Our hearts are so full with all the blessings that you have brought us. Last night you lightened our meetings with electrical light and showed us beautiful films; and today you have lightened our hearts and souls with the spiritual light of the love of Bahá'u'lláh.'

Dr Leo Neiderreiter was a medical doctor who served the people of Ethiopia including those way out in the countryside. To make it easier to get around the large country, he bought a small plane and learned to fly.

He flew Rúhíyyih Khánum to Asmara, the capital of Eritrea. At the time, Eritrea was a province of Ethiopia. Today it is an independent country. This part of the world has a lot of ancient history. Human beings have lived in this part of the world for at least 10,000 years.

Eritrea was part of the great ancient Kingdom of Aksum. Today, the whole capital of Asmara is a UNESCO World Heritage Site which means that the United Nations considers it to be of significant importance to the history and culture of the whole human race.

In Asmara, Rúhíyyih Khánum met with the Governor-General of Eritrea. He was a scholar of Eritrean culture and was telling her all about it when he cut himself off and asked about the Bahá'í Faith. He remembered that as a boy he had been in Jerusalem when Emperor Selassie was presented with a book on the Bahá'í Faith during an audience. This was quite a coincidence, Rúhíyyih Khánum said, because the Bahá'í lady at that audience was her friend, Mrs Schopflocher, who was presenting this book on behalf of her late husband, Shoghi Effendi.

After returning to Ethiopia, Rúhíyyih Khánum asked to see the famous historical sites of the country. This was easy to do because of Dr Neiderreiter's airplane. He flew her to Lalibela, Ethiopia's most famous historical site, known because of the ancient rock-cut churches there. These are built straight into the rock in the ground! The tops of the churches are at ground level so you have to walk down into the ground to go inside the church. They were built most likely by an Ethiopian king eight hundred years ago who wanted the site to be like Jerusalem, a holy city for Christians. Lalibela became a place of pilgrimage for Ethiopian Christians.

In early January, Rúhíyyih Khánum and Violette Nakhjavani set out to go by Land Rover from Uganda in east Africa all the way to Ghana in West Africa. This was almost 10,000 kilometers.* The challenge was that the roads were not well maintained, and the heavy rain in the dense forest of the Congo often made them impassable.

The Land Rover was loaded up with provisions and spare parts. The travellers had to be prepared to fix the Land Rover by themselves in the forest. They were given a crash course in a few hours on how to repair the main parts of the Land Rover. The main danger was to the underside of the Land Rover which could easily be damaged by deep potholes, tree branches, and large rocks. To prevent irreparable damage, a metal plate was put underneath the Rover.

Before they could begin their journey, they had to know which roads to take. But the Congo did not have a national highway system with road signs. They couldn't just start driving down a road in the forest—this was one of the largest and densest forests in the world. Then one day at a wedding in Kampala, Violette Nakhjavani met a Greek man who had a trading business across the border in the Congo. He knew all about the roads in eastern Congo and told her the ones to take to get to Kisangani, the capital of north-eastern Congo.

Now, Rúhíyyih Khánum, Violette Nakhjavani, and the Bahá'í Counsellor for East and Central Africa, Mr Oloro Epyeru, were all set to cross the great Congo basin and forest.

---

* 6,000 miles.

The initial roads were as difficult as they had been told. The rains had created enormous potholes, some so deep the wheel could not touch the bottom. In those cases, the travellers got out and pulled branches together to make a bridge over the hole.

Later their Land Rover came face to face with a gigantic truck transporting goods. The two could not share the road. With great difficulty Rúhíyyih Khánum got the Land Rover up on the side of the road in the bushes so the truck could get by.

The first few nights, the travellers were shown hospitality by Christian missionaries. Missionaries are people who settle in other parts of the world to serve others and teach the Christian religion. Rúhíyyih Khánum praised the energy the Christian missionaries had in teaching their faith and serving others. The missionaries were only supposed to house other Christians but they opened their homes to the Bahá'í travellers and showed them love and hospitality.

All around Rúhíyyih Khánum saw much destruction of buildings, homes, and churches. The Congolese had freed themselves of their colonisers but then violent conflict broke out between tribes and regions causing widespread death and destruction. Finally, by 1965, the country was reunified under one government.

The Congo is a vast country made up of people from many ethnic groups speaking a variety of languages. The travellers arrived in the town of Nya Nya where they came upon a small hotel. Rúhíyyih Khánum couldn't believe her eyes. This was the same one she and Shoghi Effendi had stayed in when they had crossed the Congo in 1940 going from South Africa to Egypt!

Finally, they arrived in Kisangani. Both Rúhíyyih Khánum and Violette Nakhjavani had been to this great city before. There they met Molisso Michel, a Bahá'í who had been building up the Bahá'í community there for several years. Michel travelled extensively through the villages of Burundi, a small country on Congo's eastern border.

Burundi is in the 'Great Lakes' region of Africa. The total fresh water in these bodies of water make-up twenty-five percent of the planet's unfrozen surface fresh water. The great lakes such as Lake Victoria and Lake Tanganyika are home to a great deal of biodiversity and almost ten percent of the world's fish species. Thanks to the efforts of Michel and others, numerous people became Bahá'ís.

Rúhíyyih Khánum visited villages including one where the nephew of Michel lived. Michel was the only Bahá'í in his family. There were no phones in most cases, so word had to be sent in person or by letter. Even though Michel's nephew and his family had only one day's notice that Rúhíyyih Khánum would be visiting, they worked very hard to honour her and make their home welcoming. They placed large palm leaves all along the approach to his house, prepared a delicious large meal, and went to the well to get a large basin of water for ablutions.*

Clean water is needed for the ablutions carried out before the Bahá'í obligatory prayers. In the villages, water usually had to be brought from a well. Michel's family made a lot of effort to get this

---

* The symbolic cleansing oneself by washing one's face and hands before the obligatory prayers.

water and prepare their home showing their hospitality and the great respect they had for their guests.

Leaving the Kisangani region, the travellers arrived at a broad river that could only be crossed on a ferry. But the engine of the ferry needed a large battery to spark it and get it started. The Land Rover's battery was not strong enough. So the travellers waited by the riverside for something to happen. Finally, after several hours, Rúhíyyih went around to look for a truck. When she found one, she convinced the driver to bring his truck and thanks to his battery, the ferry engine came alive, and could cross the river.

After the wide river, the road narrowed so much that there was room for only one vehicle. The jungle came right up to the Land Rover. With no place to stay, the travellers slept in abandoned buildings or ones that were not in use. When they came to the next big river, Rúhíyyih Khánum again went looking for a powerful enough battery. This time she crossed to the other side of the river by canoe looking for such a battery.

After two weeks in the dense and lush forests of the Congo, the travellers came out onto grasslands called a savannah. This was the landscape south of the great Sahara Desert. Driving across the savannah kicked up a lot of fine red dust which covered the Land Rover and the travellers. Even after several weeks, they were not able to get rid of the dust completely.

There for the first time, they met people then known as pygmies. In that part of Africa there are people who are very short and were often persecuted by their much taller neighbours. The term pygmy comes from European travellers and means dwarf. The term became generally used but is seen as pejorative today. The pygmies are actually the Bayaka, Mbuti, and Twa people of central Africa. They often lived in great poverty due in part to the prejudice that their neighbours had towards them and to the loss of their traditional forestland due to deforestation.

Rúhíyyih Khánum drove through the countries of the Central African Republic and its capital, Bangui, and Chad and its capital, Fort Lamy (today re-named N'Djamena). There, the Counsellor parted ways with his travelling companions because he had to return to Uganda. The overland trip, though, had given him a good idea of what was going on in the different communities throughout the huge region they had crossed.

From Chad, Rúhíyyih Khánum and Violette Nakhjavani turned around and began their journey towards West Africa. They arrived in the large, dry country of Niger. It was already 41 degrees Celsius* in the shade, and this was the cool season.

In the capital, Niamey, Rúhíyyih Khánum met two extraordinary pioneering families from Iran, the Djoneidis and the Sadeghzadehs. When they decided to pioneer, the women, who were home-makers from the big city of Tehran, went to Niger in advance of their husbands. They and all their children caught malaria. This disease is common in warm tropical climates where there are mosquitoes. It causes fever, chills, vomiting, and diarrhoea. Malaria can stay with a person for years with the symptoms coming and going.

---

* 105 degrees Fahrenheit

Mrs Sadeghzadeh had lost her five-year-old son to malaria. The women spoke no French—the common language of Niger, a country that had been colonised by the French. After some time, their husbands were able to join them. Though they searched, there was no work for them. The women began to make dresses and this way made a little money for the family. Rúhíyyih Khánum went with the mother to the grave of the boy who had died. The mother asked her that his death be accepted as a sacrifice for the growth of the Faith in Niger.

After meeting the Bahá'ís and the head of Niger, President Diori Hamani, a leader respected throughout Africa, Rúhíyyih Khánum drove west towards the country of Dahomey (today the country of Benin). On the way they stopped at a remote schoolhouse. The headmaster there was a Bahá'í. He was shocked when he came out and realised who was visiting him. Meeting Rúhíyyih Khánum encouraged him in his service.

Rúhíyyih Khánum drove to the countries of Dahomey and then Togo as those countries and Niger were preparing to elect the first National Spiritual Assembly of the three countries together. She helped encourage all the Bahá'ís in every village, including Dohoua which was the first place in Benin where people had become Bahá'ís. She was especially impressed by how many of the women were active and engaged in the work of the Faith.

In the fishing village of Hiye, the villagers erected a Bahá'í centre in which she spoke. The local people performed dances and music in her honour. A ten-meter pole was put up, and a dancer performed moves around it. For the finale he climbed up a pole and balanced on top of it on his stomach and then waved his arms and legs.

By the time Rúhíyyih Khánum reached Accra, the capital of Ghana, she was exhausted though exhilarated by all she had seen and experienced, especially the extraordinary sacrifice and sincerity of many Bahá'ís.

By this time she had received requests from the Universal House of Justice in her capacity as a Hand of the Cause to undertake several trips on its behalf. She and Violette Nakhjavani left West Africa in March of 1970. Violette Nakhjavani calculated that they had only completed a quarter of their intended trip even though they had travelled 12,000 miles in a little over six months. Rúhíyyih Khánum had driven the Land Rover herself over 8,000 of those miles. They would return in November.

So off they flew. They travelled to the United States, where Rúhíyyih Khánum spoke at a youth convention. Rúhíyyih Khánum represented the House of Justice at the first National Convention in Guyana, South America, for the countries of Guyana, Suriname, and French Guiana; the continental conference in La Paz, Bolivia; and to the National Convention of Ecuador. She then rested for several weeks in Panama, before going teaching from island to island in the Caribbean: Grenada, St. Vincent, Barbados, Martinique, Dominica, Guadeloupe, Antigua, St. Martin, Nevis and St. Thomas.

Rúhíyyih Khánum was surely becoming one of the most travelled women in the world!

Chapter 18

Rúhíyyih Khánum became so ill in South America that doctors told her not to return to her strenuous activities in Africa for at least two months. By 20 November, she and Violette Nakhjavani were back on the African teaching trip.

They began in Accra, Ghana, where they met dignitaries—something she did in every country she visited—and, most importantly, loaded up their Land Rover.

They drove first to Abidjan, Ivory Coast. This country is Ghana's neighbour to the west. There, Rúhíyyih Khánum found the Bahá'í community to be very active. The Bahá'ís in Abidjan met twice a week to study and then went to the villages to teach. A new Bahá'í who was a student at the local university asked her to come to his village to explain the Faith to his father who was the chief there. All the student's relatives followed the ancient traditions and gods. Belief in the traditional gods of one's ancestors and belief that gods are a manifest in the natural world is called 'animism'. This is not a particular religion like Christianity but many beliefs that a people have that date back thousands of years with no known prophet as its source or holy book like the Qur'an. There are people who hold animistic beliefs all over the world. When Rúhíyyih Khánum met the village chief she explained the Bahá'í Faith in this way:

There is one God; the God that you worship and call the Creator is the same as the God all men worship. This God has never abandoned men, His children, and always guided them through His Divine messengers. Your religion also came from God, but as it is so very old its source is lost in the mists of time. There were no written records to pass it down.[119]

The Bahá'í Faith has several teachings about religions of the past:

1. all the major known religions come originally from God and teach the same spiritual virtues, so, in reality, there is only one religion,

2. God has never left His Creation alone without spiritual guidance,

3. many Manifestations of God have appeared about whom we know nothing because they were so long ago.

From Ivory Coast, Rúhíyyih Khánum and Violette Nakhjavani continued driving west to the country of Liberia. This time, Guilda Navidi joined them. She had done such an excellent job publicising the visit to Ivory Coast that Rúhíyyih Khánum invited her to come for the rest of the second leg of this Africa teaching trip to help them.

The travellers kept driving west and arrived in the next country, Liberia, where she was going to attend the first Bahá'í Conference ever held in West Africa.

Liberia is the oldest modern nation in Africa. It was settled before 1861 by Black Americans who moved to Africa where their ancestors had originally lived and to escape the racism in the U.S. Before the Civil War in 1861, fifteen thousand Black Americans moved to Liberia and built up its capital, Monrovia.

The travellers were received by the President of the country, President Tubman, who had been to Haifa and been welcomed there by Rúhíyyih Khánum. They spoke together for a long time as friends.

Rúhíyyih Khánum also drove out to the countryside to visit Washington Farms, a National Bahá'í Endowment. George and Bessie Washington were an elderly Black American couple who had moved to Liberia, bought this piece of land, and built a large house on it for use by Bahá'ís. Rúhíyyih Khánum made a wreath of flowers and fern with her own hands and laid it on their graves and prayed.

Rúhíyyih Khánum then drove north to the country of Mali. The temperatures were well over 38 degrees Celsius.* Northern Mali is deep in the Sahara Desert. The area that is Mali today was once part of three great successive African Empires: the Empire of Ghana, the Empire of Mali, and the Empire of Songhai. These three empires controlled the trans-Saharan trade which generated enormous wealth.

The Sahara can be thought of as a sea of sand over which people have travelled for many centuries bringing goods back and forth from north Africa by long trains of camels. Though the Sahara is huge and extremely hot in the day and cold at night many people have lived there for centuries. Camel trains went from one oasis to another to make it across the vast sands. During the day there was burning heat and then when one arrived at an oasis with its trees and water, the temperature dropped way down, and one felt refreshed.

---

* 100 degrees Fahrenheit.

Rúhíyyih Khánum had always wanted to visit the city in Mali called Timbuktu, one of the most famous places in the world. The city grew rich from the trans-Saharan trade. One of its kings, Mansa Musa, made Mali an Islamic kingdom in the 1300s. Timbuktu became a centre of learning in the Islamic world. In addition to goods, there was an active trade in books. Manuscripts went out from Timbuktu to the rest of the world, and those from other places were also collected in its libraries.

From Mali, Rúhíyyih Khánum drove to Upper Volta (today's Burkina Faso) and its capital, Ouagadougou. Driving eastward over the vast distances of desert and savannah, Rúhíyyih Khánum realised how isolated Bahá'í pioneers might feel. She always lovingly encouraged them. When she spoke with local people about the Faith, she had a great ability to give them a world vision. In speaking about the Faith with a group of farmers in the village of Pagaza, she said:

When we become illumined with the light of God, we are like a candle. When we are able to form a local spiritual assembly then the light becomes greater like the light of a kerosene lamp. When many thousands accept the Faith their light will be powerful like the electric lights in the town. When the majority of the world becomes Bahá'í then their light will be like the light of the sun which illumines all. [120]

Rúhíyyih Khánum returned to Ivory Coast where the travellers had to give up their Land Rover and continue their journeys by airplane and car.

Back in Liberia, Rúhíyyih Khánum visited many small towns and villages including Bomi Hills, a strong Bahá'í community in Liberia and the oldest one. She encouraged Bahá'ís to speak to people more about the Bahá'í teachings on life after death:

> *If you have a bird who has lived in a cage all his life and one day you open the door of the cage you can see how frightened the bird is of leaving the cage. He comes to the door of the cage, he may even come out of it, but again he will go back to his cage. Several times he may hesitate at the door until he realizes he is at last free and then with joy he will fly away, higher and higher. Often the spirit of man is in the same way attached to the cage of his body and his environment and is afraid to leave them, but through the power of prayer his soul will be freed and learn to fly to its celestial home.* [121]

In Sierra Leone, Rúhíyyih Khánum met Mrs Vivian Wesson, the oldest Black American pioneer in West Africa at the time. She was a Knight of Bahá'u'lláh for having opened the country of Togo to the Bahá'í Faith with her friend, Mavis Nymon, a white American. Wesson moved to Liberia where she founded a school and was now in Sierra Leone in the care of another Bahá'í pioneer couple.

Rúhíyyih Khánum was asked to open two villages to the Bahá'í Faith. The first one was the beautiful fishing village of L'Akká. To the assembled fishermen who had come to hear her she introduced herself and the Faith this way:

If one of you goes to the sea and finds a lot of fish if you are a good man you will surely come and inform the rest of the village where the fishing is good and guide them to it. Now we have come in that same spirit to tell you of the spiritual abundance of God's grace and bounty in this day.[122]

The second village she opened was Malekei. There was a nearby high school where a boy had become a Bahá'í. The other students made fun of him for having joined an unknown religion. His teacher heard an interview with Rúhíyyih Khánum on the television and asked him if he could get her invited to the school. When Rúhíyyih Khánum arrived at the school to speak, the Bahá'í student felt proud to be a Bahá'í.

Rúhíyyih Khánum spent the next weeks in Senegal, to the west of Sierra Leone. Senegal is a mostly Muslim country with French as its official language due to its having been colonised by France. There are thirty-nine distinct languages in this country alone. Liberia has thirty-one Indigenous languages, Sierra Leone has ten, Burkina Faso has sixty-six and in Mali, seventy-nine are spoken! The foreign languages of English and French are one way people in this region speak to each other across their countries.

In the capital of Senegal, Dakar, Rúhíyyih Khánum was received by the President Leopold Senghor. He was one of the most important African thinkers of the century and a gifted poet. He promoted the idea among Africans of having a view of art and culture centred on African cultural ideas instead of those from Europe or other cultures.

Senegal has an independent country inside of it: The Gambia. This tiny country runs along the Gambia River and then touches the Atlantic Ocean. Rúhíyyih Khánum spent an exhilarating three weeks there, leading up to the holy season of Riḍván.

The local Bahá'ís organised themselves into teams and used a microbus to drive miles through different villages. One team got out at a village then the microbus continued to the next one. The driver and his team went to the last village. The Bahá'ís gathered the villagers under large trees which could provide shade and told them about the Bahá'í Faith. Then the team members got back on the microbus when it came to pick them up. The Bahá'ís were all very happy together in the bus because teaching uplifted their spirits. They shared inspiring and funny stories with each other.

One day they were driving home past a village they had not visited. An old man stood by the road side and was waving at them to stop. Everyone was tired and hungry and wanted to go home. Rúhíyyih Khánum insisted that they stop and see what the man wanted. He said that he wanted to know why they had not visited his village. Rúhíyyih Khánum got out and went to the centre of the village and spoke with him and others about the Faith until it was so dark they could no longer even see each other.

A few weeks later, it was the Festival Riḍván. This is the time that commemorates when Bahá'u'lláh declared himself as the Manifestation of God for this Day and when Bahá'ís all over the world elect their Spiritual Assemblies. Rúhíyyih Khánum was overjoyed to see how many Bahá'ís came to elect several Local Assemblies. She helped those who could not write to put down their names.

The Universal House of Justice asked Rúhíyyih Khánum to be its representative at the national convention in Abidjan to elect the National Assembly of Ivory Coast, Mali, and Upper Volta. Bahá'ís shared joyous news of the progress of the Faith in the region including the formation of a Bahá'í group in Timbuktu.

There in Abidjan they picked up their Land Rover again and packed it with supplies and drove off for a return visit to Ghana, their last country on this second leg of the Africa teaching trip. They visited many Bahá'í communities in small towns and villages and were happy to travel on land again so they could see the beautiful green hills of Ghana.

Rúhíyyih Khánum returned for the third Africa teaching trip in August 1971.

She had gone to Europe to speak to a Conference of Bahá'í youth, and then doctors insisted that she rest. The illness she had in South America was still with her.

After a month she got back on the plane and returned to Ghana with Violette Nakhjavani. They drove west into the country of Dahomey (today's Benin) where they found out they didn't have the right travel papers to go on to more countries. They were now delayed one month to wait for the new papers. But instead of complaining, Rúhíyyih Khánum got to work assisting the local Bahá'ís with their service. She gave interviews and was received by the country's highest officials.

Towards the end of the month Violette Nakhjavani got the news that her father, Musa Banani, one of the original pioneers to Uganda, had just passed away. She didn't want to leave Rúhíyyih Khánum alone, but Khánum insisted she go and honour her beloved father.

In September they arrived for the first time in the country of Nigeria, the most populous country in Africa. There are over one hundred million people in Nigeria from 250 ethnic groups speaking 500 languages! English is the common language. The three largest ethnic groups are the Hausa, Yoruba, and Igbo.

Rúhíyyih Khánum drove from West to East giving talks to hundreds of people in person and more on radio and TV. In the village of Bende, she met a large group of new Bahá'ís most of whom were women. This gave her an opportunity to speak about the importance of the role of women in society. She spoke about this whenever she could because women in many societies did not have many rights or opportunities, unlike the men.

The National Spiritual Assembly of the Bahá'ís of Nigeria had printed up thousands of posters with Rúhíyyih Khánum's picture on them to announce her visit in towns and villages. She saw them everywhere she went on trees and fences. The result was that in the villages she came to, there were hundreds of people each time waiting for her to speak to them.

She spoke in town after town—Umuasa, Ubaha, Umukwe, Itungo, Aba, Port Harcourt, Calabar, Akpabyo, and Ikotuba, the first place where the Bahá'í Faith was taught in Nigeria. In the town of Akpabyo, over a hundred men came out and accompanied Rúhíyyih Khánum for a mile doing ceremonial dances as she entered town. Women came out of their homes with a child on their backs and danced around her singing, 'Alláh'u'Abhá'.

In the beginning of October, Rúhíyyih Khánum crossed over into the country of Cameroon to the south of Nigeria. They came to the town of Mamfe which had been the original pioneering post of Hand of the Cause Enoch Olinga. He was the son of Anglican missionaries who heard about the Faith from Violette Nakhjavani's father. After becoming a Bahá'í in Uganda, he moved to Cameroon, the first Bahá'í to live there. In Cameroon, many people became Bahá'ís and then left to pioneer to other countries in Africa. Five new countries were opened to the Faith from these Bahá'ís.

Rúhíyyih Khánum headed out from Mamfe into the mountains of Western Cameroon visiting Bahá'í communities all along the way. The road got so steep at one point that they had to leave the Land Rover and walk. In one village the Bahá'ís very much wanted to have a Bahá'í centre so they built a house with mud-brick walls in the traditional way but could not afford a tin roof to protect against the rain. Gradually the rains wore down the mud brick walls and neighbours began to make fun of the Bahá'ís. They asked Rúhíyyih Khánum for assistance, and she contacted other Bahá'ís in the Cameroon who sent the funds for the roof.

Back in Mamfe, Rúhíyyih Khánum met with members of Local Assemblies throughout the area. She was especially pleased to see that the treasurers of these Assemblies were women, showing the growing role of women in the Bahá'í communities.

Rúhíyyih Khánum drove down to southern Cameroon where there had been a lot of Bahá'í teaching. In one single day she met Bahá'ís in five different villages. Bahá'ís came from all around to see her. In the village of Bakebe, the village chief greeted all the Bahá'ís who had come to see Rúhíyyih Khánum. He had on his best ceremonial robe. He said that he was an old man and could not change his religion but now that they had changed theirs, they should remain firm in their Faith.

In this one area of Cameroon there were over twenty-one Local Assemblies so Rúhíyyih Khánum stopped in numerous villages including Ebeagwa where almost everyone was Bahá'í. They gathered each morning to pray together before beginning their work for the day.

In the village of Eyang, the local people who had newly become Bahá'ís showed Rúhíyyih Khánum the large Bahá'í Centre they had built themselves in the centre of their village.

In Kumba, a teaching conference was held at which two pioneers decided to get married. Rúhíyyih Khánum gathered flowers and arranged them herself for the bride. Because the families of the bride and groom were not in Cameroon, Rúhíyyih Khánum represented the groom's family—who was American—and Violette Nakhjavani, the bride's, who was Iranian. The local people were fascinated to see the simplicity of a Bahá'í marriage which involves the exchange of one verse by the couple: 'We will all, verily, abide by the Will of God.'

This verse must be said in front of two witnesses after the parents have approved of the union.

Rúhíyyih Khánum continued to the cities of Victoria and Buea where she met the head of that region of Cameroon. He told her that it was quite extraordinary to meet two white women who had driven 34,000 kilometers* across the continent! He appreciated their interest in his country.

After a stay in Yaounde, the capital of Cameroon, and dozens of talks and interviews, Rúhíyyih Khánum drove the Land Rover onto a cargo boat to take them to the country of Zaire (today's Democratic Republic of Congo).

The trip across Zaire was 4,000 kilometers† long from west to east and took seven weeks. She spoke at thirty-eight large meetings to several thousand Bahá'ís from eighty communities. The first ten days were spent in the capital of Kinshasa which is all the way on the western edge of the country. This was a vast nation with dense forest everywhere. Fortunately Rúhíyyih Khánum was interviewed on radio, and her words were broadcast over the large distances.

When it was time to go inland, the Land Rover was loaded onto a barge going up the Zaire River (today's Congo River). The barge was pushed from behind by a large boat to which were also attached three other barges. Every inch of the barges had passengers. The accommodations went from first class to fourth class. There were people buying and selling goods eating and drinking and dancing

---

* 21,000 miles.

† 2,500 miles.

with music blasting all day and night. The whole thing was like a floating island with every kind of activity on it.

Once the boats left Kinshasa, the river became very wide like a vast lake. Going up the river, they pulled over at certain villages. Many canoes then rowed out to meet the boats and sell them fish, fruit, and meat. People actively bought and sold over the sides of the barges.

At one village, there were two Bahá'ís among those coming up to sell. One recognised the Bahá'í pioneer who was accompanying Rúhíyyih Khánum. He was showing to people around him a Bahá'í pamphlet in the local language and bringing them up to proudly introduce her to them.

The boats pulled into Port Francqui, the capital of the central province of Zaire, Kasai, an area rich in diamonds. Once Rúhíyyih Khánum drove the Land Rover off the barge and into town, smoke started coming out the engine. The hood was popped open, and they saw rags, wood shavings, paper and other items that were beginning to burn because of the heat of the engine. These items had been brought together under the hood by river rats who had built a nest for themselves for the river journey. Had they waited any longer the whole engine could have caught fire!

The Congolese Bahá'ís took their Faith and Bahá'í laws seriously. One couple learned that Bahá'ís must not drink alcohol—drinking palm wine was very common in Congo. They thought about it and reasoned that if palm wine shouldn't be drunk then they, as Bahá'ís, shouldn't even sell it. So they stopped making and selling palm wine and instead sold household items like soap and matches to light stoves. They set up a stand in front of their home. The business went so well that they gave some of their additional profit to the Bahá'í fund.

Driving down the road, it was especially exciting for the travellers to see signs saying 'Bahá'í Centre' with the name of the town next to it. Often these signs were decorated with flowers to welcome Rúhíyyih Khánum.

At a meeting in the village of Pinga Matadi, several members of the audience attempted to disrupt the meeting. There are always people who are fanatical—something Shoghi Effendi said Bahá'ís must never be—and won't listen to others, preferring to simply yell. The elderly chief was present. Though he was not a Bahá'í, he stood up and raised his hand to quiet these disruptive people. He said that the teachings of Bahá'u'lláh called for love and unity so we must listen to them. Whether to accept them or not is up to each individual.

Rúhíyyih Khánum praised the beauty of Congolese traditions. She encouraged the audience in the village of Batua Mwanda Bende to be proud of their tribal traditions. She explained that she was from a tribe in Scotland, the Maxwells, and this pleased and amused the villagers very much. Each time the first Bahá'í from a particular tribe became a Bahá'í, Shoghi Effendi would joyfully add the name to his list and announce the name to the Bahá'í world.

Villagers told Rúhíyyih Khánum of their dreams. One man beheld a figure bathed in light shining off him and soon he found the Bahá'í Faith. Another person had three successive dreams: he saw the infant Jesus in his mother's arms, the next night he was standing in a desert and the bright sun showed him the way across, and in the final dream, sunlight filled his home. Soon thereafter he found the Bahá'í Faith. Rúhíyyih Khánum's mother had many dreams that she believed were filled with meaning and that she used to guide her in life. The villagers were fascinated to hear about them.

Many of the Bahá'ís were interested to know what Bahá'u'lláh looked like. They were used to Christian churches where there were often depictions of Jesus in a statue or painting. Jesus was always depicted according to the imagination of the person making the image. Most missionaries to the Congo were from Europe so Jesus was shown as a European man. Other times Jesus was portrayed as African.

So what did Bahá'u'lláh look like? It is not permitted in the Bahá'í Faith to depict Bahá'u'lláh. There are photographs of Him but they are only shown on rare occasions such as pilgrimage. This is because the image must be treated with profound respect. However, Bahá'ís are permitted to display photos or images of 'Abdu'l-Bahá. These too should be treated with respect.

After many more village meetings with Bahá'ís and their friends, Rúhíyyih Khánum arrived in Lubumbashi, their last stop in Zaire. Located on the southern border, it's the second largest city in this vast country. There they met a long-time Congolese Bahá'í who had heard of the Faith from Rex and Mary Collision, a Canadian-American couple who were among the first from their countries to arise during the call for pioneers of the Ten-Year Crusade. They were Knights of Bahá'u'lláh for the country of Rwanda which borders Zaire. They made teaching trips into Zaire where they met a Congolese man who had been persecuted for being a Bahá'í. There had been a priest in the city denouncing the Faith and this man, who was a new Bahá'í at the time, was put in prison twice for his beliefs.

In Zambia, Rúhíyyih Khánum was invited to meet with the president of the country Kenneth Kaunda, who ruled Zambia for almost thirty years. The TV station also asked her to do a live interview. She had done many but this time, the interviewer asked that they speak more about her driving trip across Africa than the Bahá'í Faith because he had just done a show on the Faith. Within a few minutes after the interview started, though, the host became so interested in Rúhíyyih Khánum's answers that they spoke the whole time about the Faith.

Though there were forty-five Assemblies in Zambia, Rúhíyyih Khánum was prevented from visiting many of them because of the intense rains, and she became ill. Nevertheless, she roused herself, spoke to several large audiences of students, and met with as many Bahá'ís as possible.

Rúhíyyih Khánum spent most of March in Rhodesia (today's Zimbabwe), a country that was in transition from having been a colony ruled by a white minority over the native African peoples such as the Shona and the Ndebele. A local Bahá'í freed up his whole house so that Rúhíyyih Khánum could move in and recover her strength.

A Bahá'í teacher, Mr Laurence Hautz, who ran a school for children free of charge on his property, had a three-month old infant who died. Rúhíyyih Khánum spoke words of comfort at the funeral.

Over one-hundred children came each with a flower in their hand. The Bahá'í prayer for the dead was read in the Shona language. This prayer is the only Bahá'í prayer that is said all together. It consists of six verses repeated by everyone nineteen times and, in between, the Greatest Name is repeated. Rúhíyyih Khánum always encouraged Bahá'ís in different countries to have this prayer translated into local languages because its effects were powerful. The grandmother at this funeral was so moved by what she heard that she became a Bahá'í.

Her official visit to Bahá'í communities throughout the countries would have to be delayed. Again now, her duties as a Hand of the Cause called her, and she had to leave this leg of the Africa teaching trip.

Chapter 19

Rúhíyyih Khánum and Violette Nakhjavani left Africa for a few months so she could attend certain events and conferences at the request of the Universal House of Justice. Among the highlights of this time was the dedication of the first Bahá'í temple in Central America which was built in Panama, a Bahá'í community that was thriving.

The temple built in Panama was the first Bahá'í House of Worship in Central or South America. Rúhíyyih Khánum flew there to dedicate it in April 1972. She and Hands of the Cause Ugo Giachery and Zikrullah Khadem were there representing the Universal House of Justice.

British architect Peter Tillotson designed the temple. The nine-pointed star has points built of walls that are made of local stone in pattern like those made by Indigenous people in the pre-Columbian period (the years before the arrival of Christopher Columbus). The temple site is on top of a high mountain that overlooks Panama City, the capital of the country. The top of the mountain had to be flattened so that the temple could be built there.

〜

When Rúhíyyih Khánum and Violette Nakhjavani returned to Africa, they spent one month in the southern African country of Rhodesia (today's Zimbabwe). She drove the Land Rover to many villages where the Bahá'ís told her that what they really wanted was to build schools.

One of the most important chiefs in Rhodesia, Chief Nemangwe, was a Bahá'í. He invited Rúhíyyih Khánum to his village. There he acted as a judge for the area and had his own court house. Rúhíyyih Khánum and her companions stayed in a room next to the courthouse and used the main room for cooking and meeting people. They put their portable stove on the riser where the judge sat and ate at the main table.

In front of the courthouse was a large awning made of thatch under which people could come and discuss their cases out of the blazing sun. There Rúhíyyih Khánum met and spoke with the local Bahá'ís. They discussed life after death at great length. The chief was fascinated to learn of the Bahá'í teaching that this life is a preparation for the next one. He and the sub-chief in the next village both donated land for Bahá'í centres.

From Rhodesia, Rúhíyyih Khánum drove south into Botswana. This country is much more arid than Rhodesia because much of it is in the Kalahari Desert. In addition to visiting Bahá'ís in numerous village communities, Rúhíyyih Khánum was eager to meet the Kalahari bushmen, or San people as outsiders also call them. These Indigenous people speak Khoe, Tuu, or Kx'a languages, and were made famous beyond South Africa by British documentaries about them. They were hunter-gatherers until recently and have lived in southern Africa for over 20,000 years.

Rúhíyyih Khánum drove for four days throughout this region and was fortunate to be accompanied by the Chairman of the National Spiritual Assembly of the Bahá'ís of Botswana who was a linguist and could speak with the people of the Kalahari. Because they are semi-nomadic, it was difficult to find groups of them. A guide helped the visitors follow a footpath through high dry grass. This led them to an encampment of bushmen who danced and sang to welcome their visitors. In this settlement they lived without even shelter, living off hunting with their bows and arrows and gathering grain.

For Rúhíyyih Khánum, this was a fascinating experience because here were people who had been living and thriving in the desert for thousands of years and were only somewhat aware of the outside world. They were also famous for their elaborate cave paintings. Rúhíyyih Khánum was moved by their gentleness.

A missionary in Botswana asked Rúhíyyih Khánum if only literate people could become Bahá'ís because the Faith had no clergy, and clergy were usually the only ones who read holy books and explained them to regular people. Rúhíyyih Khánum answered:

Bahá'u'lláh has brought the principle of universal education and we see clearly in the world today that the circumstances of civilization are making it possible to eliminate illiteracy all over the world in one or two generations. But faith and recognition of the truth from God is not dependent upon book learning. There are two doors through which people can recognize spiritual truth; the door of mind or intellect and the door of the heart or intuition. [123]

From Botswana, Rúhíyyih Khánum drove south into the Republic of South Africa. The border city in South Africa was Mafeking which she knew about because of Hand of the Cause John Robarts who had been the first Bahá'í to settle in that region and was named a Knight of Bahá'u'lláh by Shoghi Effendi. Robarts was a Canadian Bahá'í who travelled the world teaching the Faith and settled in South Africa during the Ten-Year Crusade.

During the 1970s, South Africa still enforced the apartheid system of racial segregation. Apartheid separated people by race such that certain areas, schools, jobs, and rights were for whites only, and black Africans had to have special passes to go places. Despite this system, black and white Bahá'ís found ways of associating with one another.

Rúhíyyih Khánum was fortunately able to meet Bahá'ís of all races. Apartheid had a racial class of citizens labelled 'coloured' that included people of South and East Asian descent as well as people from a variety of races. Rúhíyyih Khánum visited the 'coloured' towns of Eersterus, Stellenbosch, and Bredasdorp. There was a white-owned estate that was so impressed by the 'coloured' employees who were Bahá'ís that they allowed them to invite Black African friends to meetings there.

The Republic of South Africa contains within it an entire independent country: Lesotho. In this rural and mountainous country, one can see the elaborate cave art of the San people. King Motlot-lehi Moshoeshoe II invited Rúhíyyih Khánum to meet with him. She praised his country and expressed her appreciation of the openness of the African peoples she had met on her long journeys across the continent. At the end of the audience, she gave him a gift that she had personally wrapped in silk in the traditional Iranian way. The King had been to Iran and was delighted. He asked Rúhíyyih Khánum to wrap it up again so that his wife could have the same pleasure in opening it.

Rúhíyyih Khánum visited Bahá'ís in the villages. Most of these were built on mountaintops. The weather gets quite cold there, so she had to wear two blankets while speaking to people. Many of the villages were ruled by female chiefs, several of whom were Bahá'ís. A woman could become a chief if her husband was a chief and died before her.

When Rúhíyyih Khánum was nearing the village of Liphaleng, several residents rode out on horses to meet her. She asked if she could ride a horse into town. The villagers were delighted to see their distinguished visitor come in on a horse. Liphaleng overlooked a deep valley which was the ancestral home of the king. Everyone including the elderly chieftainess came out to hear her. She looked out over the mountains and used the valley at night as an image for heaven and hell:

Last night this sun set and an icy chill gripped the earth. The sun was not here and we felt its absence keenly and yearned for it. Now that the sun is out again, we are all so happy, enjoying its warmth that enters our body and fills our being. God is like this sun; our souls yearn to be near Him and partake of His life-giving love. Hell is as if, when the sun has set and one is freezing cold, one is not even allowed to enter a hut and warm oneself by the fire; therefore hell is that condition of knowing of the heat, longing to bask in the sunlight of God's good pleasure and love, but because of one's own actions in this life, unable to get near it. Heaven is that blissful state of nearness to our Creator, our goal and our eternal beloved. [124]

In the village of Belos, the well-known eighty-year-old chieftainess, Mamazibuku, hosted the travellers with a delicious meal of mutton. Neighbouring villagers came. There was a lot of dancing to entertain the guests. Mamazibuku, who had a great sense of humour, then gave Rúhíyyih Khánum a jar of homemade jam. She said that now they were married, and this was their wedding treat. Rúhíyyih Khánum was surprised by this. She said:

'Well, that is very interesting, but if you and I are married are you the bridegroom?'

Mamazibuku answered 'You are the bridegroom and I am the bride.'

Rúhíyyih Khánum smilingly said: 'Why should I be the bridegroom? After all, this marriage is your idea, not mine!' [125]

Both then broke out in laughter. The Chieftainess was honouring Rúhíyyih Khánum with this gesture.

Rúhíyyih Khánum visited the village of Seqonoka, the hometown of the first person to become a Bahá'í in Lesotho. The Bahá'ís there showed her the home where Frederick and Elizabeth Laws lived. They were the Knights of Bahá'u'lláh for this country that was known back in the 1950s as 'Basutoland'. The Laws lived an extraordinary life of service to the Bahá'í Faith, pioneering in several countries in Africa and back in the United States on the Omaha Indian Reservation in Nebraska. During this time in Lesotho, over seventy local people became Bahá'ís and seven Local Spiritual Assemblies were founded.

In this village an individual asked Rúhíyyih Khánum why there were multiple Manifestations of God. An elderly man stood and said that in their village the chief asks a different man each time to send a message he has for the villagers so is the important thing the man or the message?

The village of Thaba Bosiu, near the capital, had a unique Bahá'í community. It had a Spiritual Assembly made up of all women. Rúhíyyih Khánum remarked that wherever there were strong, devoted Bahá'í women, the community would be strong and stable.

Among the most devoted Bahá'ís in Lesotho were those who lived high up in the northern mountains. Rúhíyyih Khánum drove the Land Rover through terrifying mountain passes to an altitude above 3,000 metres.* The travellers arrived at the village of Thaba-Li-Mpe, a

---

* 10,000 feet.

group of huts that was six miles from the nearest town. Snow covered the ground. The temperature was very cold. To heat themselves villagers had to use animal dung because there were no trees for burning wood. The problem with this method is that the smoke and smell make one's eyes water and the dung burns out quickly. But the villagers had no choice if they wanted warmth.

The Bahá'ís held a day-long conference with their guests. Over eighty people attended. People came from as far as twenty miles on foot and horseback. Many women came on foot with babies. Bahá'í travel teachers rarely came to this area because of its inaccessibility. Still there were several functioning Local Assemblies.

A man showed up almost frozen from the cold. He said his wife had just given birth to a son. He asked Rúhíyyih Khánum if he could name the newborn 'Shoghi Effendi'. Rúhíyyih Khánum suggested the name 'Rabbani' instead, Shoghi Effendi's family name. The man was extremely happy and decided to name his child Rabbani.

An elderly woman arrived late at night extremely tired and cold. She had walked fifteen miles through mountain passes. The year before, she had been a delegate to the National Bahá'í Convention of Lesotho and still wore her identification badge with pride. Violette Nakhjavani took her in her arms and said that she must be very tired. The woman smiled and answered that the distance she had come was nothing compared to that of the distinguished guests. She asked that if the love of the guests for them was so great they would travel thousands of miles, why wouldn't her love for Bahá'u'lláh be such that she would walk a short distance?

To return to South Africa, Rúhíyyih Khánum steered the Land Rover down the Sani Pass. This is the highest pass on the continent and is known as the roof of Africa. The unpaved road makes dozens of hairpin turns so one must drive extremely carefully to not go off the road and plunge one thousand metres. Several times Rúhíyyih Khánum had to back up and go forward multiple times to get around a single turn. Only four by four vehicles—not regular cars—could handle such a road. Before attempting the dangerous drive, Rúhíyyih Khánum rode a horse down a section of the road to scout it out.

From South Africa, Rúhíyyih Khánum went to Swaziland (today's Eswatini), a small landlocked country on the western border with Mozambique. Though it is one of the smallest countries in Africa, it has a great deal of biodiversity and landscapes such as mountains, savannahs, and forests.

Sobhuza II, the king of Swaziland, invited Rúhíyyih Khánum to meet with him. He asked her about the Faith and its teachings about other religions. The king had 200 wives and asked about polygamy, the practice of marrying more than one woman. Rúhíyyih Khánum explained that the Bahá'í teaching was that marriage should be monogamous but that if someone became a Bahá'í who already had more than one wife, they would not be forced to divorce as this would be unjust.

The next day, the visitors were invited to watch a special presentation of the reed dance in which young, unmarried women danced dressed in beads and holding a long reed. The princesses had red feathers in their hair splayed out like a fan.

One of the princesses then came up to invite Rúhíyyih Khánum to dance with them in front of everyone. She did not want to offend her hosts, so she kicked off her sandals and danced with the young ladies.

Rúhíyyih Khánum was also invited to participate and speak at several official events attended by most of the influential people in the Swazi government. They were pleased to hear her positive thoughts on the great destiny of Africa.

The next country Rúhíyyih Khánum wanted to visit was Malawi which is north of Mozambique. The roads were not good enough for the very long drive, so she decided to put the Land Rover on a boat going up the east coast of Africa to Kenya and take a plane from there to Malawi. By pure coincidence, the captain was the same captain of the boat that had brought the travellers down the west coast of Africa in 1970.

The President of Malawi, Dr Banda, invited Rúhíyyih Khánum to meet with him. He proudly showed a gift he had received from Enoch Olinga who had visited him before. The gift was a plaque with a lion's head and a quotation from the Bahá'í Writings.

The village of Mpaso had a new Bahá'í community which included several older people. They asked Rúhíyyih Khánum if she was saying that they should leave their churches and go to a new one. She explained that the Bahá'í Faith was not a new church to add to the other churches but the Message of God for this day, the fulfilment of all the religions of the past.

She then shared her understanding of the power of prayer. Bahá'ís, she explained, used the greeting, 'Alláh'u'Abhá,' which is itself a prayer. Had it not been for this short prayer, she would not have succeeded in making these long journeys across Africa because they encountered many difficulties. The audience was so excited to hear this that they wanted the term 'Alláh'u'Abhá' written on all their pamphlets so they could learn it.

Rúhíyyih Khánum noticed that in many towns and villages she visited in Malawi, Bahá'ís were building and taking great care of their local centre. She saw that often there was a colour photograph of the Shrine of the Báb on the wall. She was informed that deepening classes had taken place nationally, and these photographs given to participants. When they returned to their homes, they wanted to use them to beautify their Bahá'í centres. Many of these centres were built by the local believers and included brick floors and flowers planted outside showing the great care they took of their Bahá'í centres.

In the town of Amalika, the Bahá'í community of Malawi purchased a beautiful National Teaching Institute with a large main hall, dormitories, and a garden. This Institute made it possible to train teachers of the Faith who could go to all regions of the country.

From Malawi, Rúhíyyih Khánum flew to the Seychelles Islands, an archipelago of 115 islands in the Indian Ocean to the east of the continent of Africa. Its population is a mix of African, Indian, Chinese, and British, and is the smallest of any African country.

There were two Bahá'í centres in the islands, the National Centre and one in the town of Anse Aux Pins. There were several large families of Bahá'ís on these islands. The property for this centre was donated by one of them. There was very little available land. The

Bahá'ís built a small centre on this land behind a shop owned by the father. He received many offers to rent his shop because of the lack of land on the island but he would do so only on the condition that no alcohol be sold there. The selling and use of alcohol is contrary to the Bahá'í teachings, and too much drinking of alcohol was a big problem in the Seychelles.

Rúhíyyih Khánum had the opportunity to visit a grove of rare palm trees that originate in the Seychelles, *coco de mer*. These palm trees have the largest nuts of any tree in the world. When they washed up on shore on other islands people did not know what to make of them. All kinds of beliefs arose about where they came from. Since the large nuts couldn't float, they sank to the bottom of the ocean. After some time, the water caused the husk to fall off, and the nuts floated to the surface. Among many other myths, people thought they grew on the bottom of the ocean. These trees are only found on this island so the government of the Seychelles guards them very closely as the trees cannot be replaced.

From the Seychelles, Rúhíyyih Khánum flew to Kenya and drove back for one more visit to Zaire. This time their visit was concentrated in the eastern province of Kivu which bordered the countries of Rwanda and Burundi which they visited before and after Zaire. This province had the most Bahá'ís in Zaire, numbering at that time possibly as many as 30,000.

These numerous Bahá'ís were, in a sense, the fruits of the teaching work of Rex and Mary Collison and their interpreter and co-worker, Dunduzu Chisza, a Bahá'í from Malawi. The Bahá'ís remained strong, and their communities grew even amid the violence of civil war and faced with opposition from churches. By the time Rúhíyyih Khánum arrived in Kivu in her Land Rover, there were 600 Local Spiritual Assemblies.

In the strong communities of the region of Fizi in southern Kivu, the Bahá'ís suffered terribly. Many people were at the mercy of roving armed groups and had to live and hide in the forest for their own protection. A Bahá'í man's eight-year-old son was shot and killed by armed men.

The homes of local Bahá'ís were already too crowded with family to accommodate the travellers, and there were no hotels. Fortunately, the Christian missions showed them hospitality. They spent three nights in a mission school run by Catholic nuns in the town of Uvira. Since it was Christmas time, the students had all gone home to their villages. Though the large empty dormitories were eerie at night with the sound of bats flying up near the roof, the travellers were grateful for the shelter. On New Year's Eve 1972, they had dinner with the Catholic Bishop in the town of Kasai and now, in 1973, they were dining with the Catholic nuns of Uvira.

A general meeting was called in the village of Ngovi in the Fizi district. Hundreds of Bahá'ís came streaming towards the village including many who walked down from the mountains on foot, one group from eighty miles. Many of the mountain villages were practically cut off from the valley because of the difficulty of travel, so only recently found out about the gathering. Once they came down from the mountains, they protested at having been left out, but the problem was the difficulty in communication. Even the bridge to cross the river to get to the village was quite broken down and risky.

To protect against the sun, five rows of nine poles, five yards apart, were planted and then large palm leaves were spread out on top. Even this was not quite enough, and the sun's hot rays pierced through any openings, so every once in a while one of the ladies would remove an outer skirt and spread the material over the leaves. Soon the meeting was protected from the sun by many pieces of colourful material!

The Bahá'ís of the Fizi region were a great source of spiritual strength for the Bahá'ís of Zaire. Many had suffered persecution for having become Bahá'ís but they persevered out of love for the Faith. The communities had grown and become strong without any assistance from the outside.

Inspired once again by the Congolese Bahá'ís, Rúhíyyih Khánum drove back to Kenya through Burundi, stopping long enough to meet with the devoted Egyptian pioneer couple there, and then on through Tanzania and back to Nairobi, Kenya. At the National Bahá'í Centre there, a large gathering was held to say goodbye to Rúhíyyih Khánum and Violette Nakhjavani and to hear parting words of wisdom.

Rúhíyyih Khánum and Violette Nakhjavani had covered over 30,000 miles in their Land Rover, by airplane, and on foot, meeting extraordinary Bahá'ís all along the way and learning a great deal about the vibrant cultures of Africa. Shoghi Effendi had crossed this continent twenty years earlier.

Rúhíyyih Khánum's title, by which she was often referred, was Amatu'l-Bahá meaning Handmaiden of Glory. She was the last living link to the holy family of the Bahá'í Faith. She helped to uplift the hearts and visions of the Bahá'ís in more than thirty countries of Africa.

Before going to Africa for the first time, she went to pray at the grave of Shoghi Effendi in London. On her way back to Haifa after an absence of more than three and half years, she once again went to bow her head in gratitude at the resting place of her beloved husband.

When asked about her trip and its physical challenges she said:

I am a widow, sixty-two years old; I have no children, no sisters, no brothers, no parents. The only reason I have come to Africa, at this age, is in response to the beautiful words of 'Abdu'l-Bahá, and because the only time the beloved Guardian gave any indication of what I might do after him, was one day, when suddenly, he looked at me and said, 'What will become of you after I die …?' This distressed me very much and I pleaded with him not to say such a terrible thing, that I would never live after he was dead; but he continued and said, 'I suppose you will go and visit the friends in different countries and encourage them.' If I can do this at my age, of course you can do it too. [126]

Chapter 20

Rúhíyyih Khánum crossed Africa and South Asia by foot, car, train, and plane. She inspired and educated Bahá'ís in cities, small towns, and remote villages alike.

But she was nowhere near finished with travelling the world for the Faith.

The Bahá'í communities in Latin America were growing rapidly in the 1960s and 70s. To reach out to the Indigenous people, Rúhíyyih Khánum decided to make an extraordinary journey in 1975. She had travelled in the air and on the ground but this time she would go a whole new way: by water.

The Amazon is the largest river in the world. It discharges more water into the ocean than the next seven largest rivers in the world *combined*. Twenty percent of all the river water that flows into the ocean is from the Amazon.

North of the Amazon is another mighty river: the Orinoco, the fourth largest river in the world and one of the longest; flowing through the countries of Colombia, Venezuela, and Suriname where many Indigenous people lived along it in lush forests. Rúhíyyih Khánum believed that Shoghi Effendi would have wanted her to make a special effort to meet Indigenous people all over the world.

The best way to do that in this case seemed to be to make a great river journey up the Orinoco.

Masud Khamsi, a devoted Bahá'í from Iran who was serving as a Bahá'í Counsellor in South America helped organise this extraordinary trip. They began in the country of Venezuela which borders the Atlantic Ocean.

They called the trip the Green Light Expedition.

Here is this amazing voyage recounted in Rúhíyyih Khánum's own words:

'The small Bahá'í community of Puerto Ayacucho met us at the airport and helped us load our provisions onto the truck. It took us over an hour to reach Venado a huge flat hunk of rock into the Orinoco river. This is the place where all traffic above Puerto Ayacucho leaves for the interior. Some weeks previous to our arrival, Mr. Khamsi had rented a large river barge which was waiting for us and for our 60 pieces of equipment, baggage and provisions.

This was the ship that was going to take us 1700 km to visit 8 different Indian tribes in the interior. This is to be our home for 32 nights and we named her the Queen Mary. The little white room at the back was our bathroom.

On the Venezuelan part of our journey we were accompanied throughout by Leco Zamora, a Mataco Indian pioneer from

Argentina. *Every evening our boat was moored on a sand bank for the night. Our first job in the morning was to roll up our hammocks and get them out of the way. Life aboard the Queen Mary was in no way difficult. In fact, the only real inconvenience were the black flies which in this particular moment were so vicious that I wore my mosquito net hat.*

Wonderful as the water was for drinking it was usually very dangerous to swimming. The [Indigenous people] always seemed to know where is safe to go in and our captain strongly advised the men that they should only bathe from the rocks. We soon found out why. I caught three man-eating piranha fish in less than two minutes.

Every morning we held prayers for the success of our expedition and that we would be guided to do the right thing and meet the right people during the day. Along the Orinoco River and also in the neighbourhood of Puerto Ayacucho itself there are a great many Bahá'í communities …

Over and over again after we had had prayers we found that the door would open in the most remarkable ways for us to meet the people that we wanted to see.

The Piaroa [...] invited us to their village,† as it was an hour's walk from the river they agreed to come back and take us there

---

* The Mataco or Wichi are a group of tribes that speak the same language and live in Argentina and Bolivia.

† The Piaroa are an Indigenous people who have lived in the Orinoco River

the following morning. [They] invited us to hold a meeting in the local schoolhouse and to tell them about our teachings. I am very happy that I could come and see them.

In the whole Amazonian Territory of Venezuela the most important town after Puerto Ayacucho is San Fernando which was founded over 200 years ago by missionaries and was very much like an old-fashioned colonial town. Although I do not attend church services I like very much when I am travelling to go into churches to pray that the people of the area in which I am travelling and teaching, may be guided to the message of Bahá'u'lláh.

Three days later we reached Laventa Rosa which to our own joy we discovered it is an entirely Bahá'í village. These people have migrated up to the river and taken enough land and established themselves. They took us and showed us where they planned to build their local Bahá'í Centre. They had already set aside this piece of land with this object in view.

Now we entered the Bentuari (river) which is much narrower and shallower than the Orinoco. Because of this, we found that we very often got grounded on sandbars and it was necessary for all of us to get out and push. The captain took no more chances and picked the channel himself very carefully.

---

basin for possibly thousands of years. They refer to themselves as the Huottüja, which in their language means 'knowledgeable people of the forest'.

Yuca, which is known in other countries as cassava or manioc, is the universal staple of the [Indigenous people] throughout South America in the jungles. [The staple food of the jungle people of South America is yucca, known also as manioc or cassava. It is first grated, the pulp put into a woven tube and compressed to extract the bitter juice, then rubbed through sieves ... and the resulting coarse flour roasted over a fire and eaten as meal or made into flat, dry, hard cakes of bread which will keep for some time.] We found the [Indigenous people to be] extraordinarily friendly people. If you met them with an open heart and a friendly spirit you immediately received the same response. We were able in many of the villages to purchase papayas, bananas and even fresh eggs.

As our boat could not navigate in the shallow waters of the tributaries, we hired a dugout canoe and installed our own outboard motor, and used it for side trips.

We made a special trip up the Manapiare river to visit the growing town of San Juan of Manapiare ... San Juan is the government outpost and an active centre for missionaries ... We met two Americans who belonged to an Evangelical group called The New Tribes Mission. One of them had just flown in for a visit to see how the work was progressing. The other had lived in Venezuela with his wife and children for over 20 years.

We also met the Catholic father, a Jesuit priest from Spain ... The people themselves of the tribes talk to their own people, more clearly, better, more concisely than we do, but the pioneers have prestige. When we go with Leco, Leco can teach better ...

We met a Piaroa Chief. We invited him aboard our boat to have coffee. He said that fifteen years before he would have been afraid to go on a boat that was owned by white men ... this shows how much people are changing. It also shows how the spirit of the Bahá'ís gives people confidence. He was a widower whose wife had died when their last child was born and he was bringing up a group of small children himself. The attachment of the children to the father and the extraordinary tenderness that he showered upon his children was very, very touching ... We discovered that eight years ago the Piaroa Chief was already in contact with some of the Bahá'ís ... If a man such as this accepts Bahá'u'lláh's teachings he will not only be a very fine believer but instrumental in bringing in many, many of his people into the Cause of God.

The Makos as a tribe have never been converted to Christianity. We were fortunate to meet their more important chief, who called a meeting to hear about the Faith ...

Finally we reached the waterfalls at Tangua. This was the furthest the Queen Mary could go. We were told that beyond the falls, there was an island called Monotiti where we could contact one of the most interesting and primitive tribes in Venezuela and Brazil called the Yanomamos. We walked about thirty kilometres on this one trip. It was the longest walk of my entire life. [The Yanomamo grow and spin the cotton to make thread for their beautiful, cool hammocks, such as the one this woman is weaving] [They] have the custom of sucking a plug of tobacco stuck in their lower lip.

Fundamentally, unity in diversity which is such a strong principle in the Bahá'í Teachings means that we are all alike and are all different ...

The second part of our trip took place in Suriname where we went to visit people of [African-Indigenous descent who lived in the Amazon forest] ... We arrived at the village of Redi Doti ... No Bahá'ís have been into the interior before to visit [them] ...

... many of [them] still follow the old [animistic religious beliefs] of Africa. Many of the homes have a small shrine in front of them to protect the people from evil spirits. Voodoo as it is called in our part of the world, JuJu as it is called in West Africa, means magic. Sometimes the people held religious services of their own which we did not intrude upon. The headman, or captain of the village, very kindly placed their meeting hall at our disposal – and we were able to live in it during the period of our visit to Reddi Dotie ...

On the second part of our visit to [them] ... we flew over the Suriname river on our way to Boto Passi. We loaded all our things on a canoe and went upriver to the Kamaloea where we were to meet our Bahá'í friends. We were received with great warmth and hospitality by Bahá'ís and non-Bahá'ís alike.

Our visit to Kamaloea was one of the warmest experiences on the whole Green Light Expedition. We had a special meeting the night of our arrival and the captain of the village, or chief, was very anxious to hear more about the Bahá'í teachings.

The next morning we discussed with our Bahá'í friends how we could best help their teaching work. They are speaking Taki Taki which is the language most commonly used in Suriname and is similar to pidgin English …

We decided to visit the nearby village of Lafanti and hold a meeting there. A number of people accepted the Faith. The people of African-Indigenous descent make their own canoes by the same method used in Africa, curing them with both fire and water. This village was the most beautiful I have ever been to in my entire life.

We decided to hold the election of the first Spiritual Assembly of Kamaloea which would be the first Spiritual Assembly of people of [African-Indigenous descent] anywhere in Suriname. As this Bahá'í could not be present at the evening meeting, he cast his vote and Jamshid wrote it down for him … Plans were made for the election of the Spiritual Assembly that night. The captain who in meantime had become a Bahá'í is casting his vote for the first Spiritual Assembly. Some of our Bahá'í friends took us down the river. On our way down river we stopped at this village to see if we could see the only Bahá'í who lived there. Although everybody else was out working their plantations, he happened to be at home.

We were nine hours on our way down the river from Kamaloea to Mamadam. Mamadam is the place where the government ferryboat picks up passengers twice a week and takes them over to Afobaka on the other side of the lake. This is to be our home for three nights where we slept with about 40 other passengers waiting for the arrival of the ferryboat. That night our Bahá'í friends cooked dinner for us – a delicious soup of piranha and plantain.

Some of the people living in the hut were very anxious to know more about the Bahá'í Faith. Our friends from Kamaloea were very enthusiastic teachers. After discussing the Faith practically the entire night with our friends, this man expressed the wish to become a Bahá'í and Jamshid enrolled him the morning of our departure. These ... Bahá'í's of [African descent] were amongst the finest that I have ever met anywhere in the world and we parted from each other with great regret. Our Bahá'í brothers embarked in their canoe and went back up the river to Kamaloea. Everything was loaded onto the crowded government ferry and we set out for the five-hour journey across the lake. We found marked interest from our fellow passengers in who we were and in what we believed.

Brazil – Manaus

We flew over the Amazon river which at this point was over 20 kilometers wide. The whole area was flooded because the rainy season had begun. It was a great revelation to all of us to discover that Manaus, in the heart of the Amazon Basin was such a modern city with shipping in its ports from all parts of the world ... We arrived to attend the first historic Bahá'í conference of the Amazonian region and were greeted very warmly at the airport by members of the new Bahá'í community. During our week's visit there were many lectures given to students at both universities and high schools.

Colombia – Leticia

From Manaus we flew to Leticia in Colombia on the frontier between Brazil and Peru ...

Boats on the Amazon are enclosed because of the very heavy rains. For eighteen days ten of us lived and slept on this one. She was noisy, smelly and slow. We called her, appropriately, the Mutt. This was the beginning of our journey up the Amazon in Peru. Gradually a daily pattern of living on the boat was established ... The rainy season floods the riverbanks but the villagers are used to it and build their homes on stilts reaching their homes by canoe. Various Christian missions are rapidly spreading throughout this entire area.

The only quiet place [in the boat] was the roof where we held prayers every morning. It was also the only place where we could have a conversation because the noise of the diesel engine inside was absolutely deafening. The trouble was that it was very difficult to get up and down because there was no deck on our boat ...

We had expected the Amazon River to be a wild and unpopulated area and we were very surprised to find that all along the riverbank there were villages and settlements ... The Amazon is the land of mirror images – one glides through a dream of exquisite beauty.

In search of [Indigenous people] left untouched by our civilization we went up the smaller rivers. We'd at last come to this Yagua* family living according to their own customs. The Yagua are a very quiet people, a very restful people, who think before they speak. They have a dignity and a nobility which constantly impressed us. No people tame wild animals like [they did]. Their homes are full of much loved and cared for pets. When the time comes for me to have to leave this planet, the only thing that is going to be the hardest to depart is from the jungles. I have this mad, mad love for the jungles. I never feel that I can see enough of the jungle, be in the jungle enough, and whenever in my life I travel away from the jungle

---

* The Yagua are Indigenous people who live in Colombia and northeastern Peru. Their name comes from Quechua, the language of the Inca, and may refer to the red paint they sometimes use on their faces.

area, it is infinite heartache that I'm leaving this marvelous, marvelous land of trees and of nature, and the beauty.

Going deeper into the jungle we came to another more isolated Yagua village ... We went back to the Amazons and visited another Yagua village.

Going up another river we visited the Bora tribe. This huge hut, called a Cocomera, is the meeting house for the villagers. We decided to go upstream, a day's journey, to see a Cocomera in another village which was still being used as a communal dwelling. In the Bahá'í teachings there is a tremendous emphasis on the family, on respect for parents, mutual kindness and understanding. This is something that exists in villages.

Peru – Iquitos and Pucallpa

Our journey to the Amazon was at an end. We are approaching Iquitos, an inland port, 4 000 km from the sea. Recently, oil has been discovered in this part of the world. To cities such as this the Indigenous people flock in great numbers, only to live in squalor and poverty. The filth produced by modern towns flows into the riverbanks. Here in Pucallpa many poor people have built their houses floating on the river itself.

We decided to visit the Shipibo* people who are both very gifted artistically and also very shrewd. The women wear very

---

* Shipibo are Indigenous people of the Amazon; they are the third largest group in the Peruvian Amazon, with 36,000 people and over 150 communities.

beautiful, embroidered skirts. To me it is very impressive the way in village life even very small children work, and they love working …

Bolivia – Oruro

The last stage of the Green Light Expedition took place on the Altiplano in the Andes. We went to Bolivia to attend a Bahá'í conference [for Indigenous peoples]. The friends gathered from many towns and villages all over the Altiplano. From Sacaca we set out for the top of the mountains accompanied by about 150 Bahá'ís. Each group of Bahá'ís villagers had brought their own instruments. Almost all of them played their flutes all the way up to the top of the mountain …

Peru – Cusco

… We arrived in Cusco, the ancient capital of the Inca Empire, to attend the first all Quechua speaking conference ever to be held which had been arranged by the Counselors of South America. Many of the Bolivian Bahá'ís had come to attend. It took this bus load of Bahá'ís from Ecuador over a week to drive the 2 000 kms from their country to Cusco. The Andean believers flocked to register for the conference. The Bahá'ís from Peru, Ecuador and Bolivia spent one whole day discussing how much they could understand each other's dialects so that Bahá'í literature could be made standard for all these countries.

It was a colourful group of people who gathered at Sacsayhuaman for the opening day of our conference. This great fortress built by the Incas took 30,000 people 80 years to construct. We went up to the highest point to hold our meeting, the place where the Incas believed the sun was tied ... Macchu Pichu was a fortress hanging in the clouds. Built by the Incas over 500 metres above the valley below. We all came by train from Cusco to visit this famous place, one of the last strongholds of the Inca empire. We held our meetings and prayers again on the spot where the sun is tied. The first mass conversion in the Western hemisphere began in Bolivia, how much joy it brought to the heart of the Guardian. I remember how he announced it to the Bahá'í world and how thrilled we were. And now here was a Bolivian Bahá'í addressing other Andean Bahá'ís at the top of the historic Machu Picchu.'[127]

This long and magnificent river journey through the lush jungles of the Amazon made a great impression on Rúhíyyih Khánum. She was greeted with openness and warmth by Indigenous people everywhere. They were very trusting and kind, and Rúhíyyih Khánum believed that they would be open and receptive to the teachings and ideas of the Bahá'í Faith. She hoped Bahá'ís would respond to 'Abdu'l-Bahá's call and travel among them:

O that I could travel, even though on foot and in the utmost poverty, to these regions, and, raising the call of 'Yá Bahá'u'l-Abhá' in cities, villages, mountains, deserts and oceans, promote the divine teachings! This, alas, I cannot do. How intensely I deplore it! Please God, ye may achieve it.[128]

In 1973, the Universal House of Justice established a new Bahá'í Institution: The International Teaching Centre. The Hands of the Cause had been appointed by Shoghi Effendi to encourage the teaching of the Faith and to protect the Bahá'í community from attacks and division. The Bahá'í community had grown since the 1950s so there was much more work to do! The International Teaching Centre was created to oversee the teaching and protection of the Faith. The Hands of the Cause and three Counsellors were appointed to the first group of the International Teaching Centre.

The Hands of the Cause, the Counsellors, and the members of the Auxiliary Board are the *appointed* arm of the Bahá'í Administrative Order. The other branch—the National and Local Spiritual Assemblies—is the *elected* arm. The Universal House of Justice is elected and is the head of both branches.

In her role as Hand of the Cause, Rúhíyyih Khánum was a member of the International Teaching Centre. One of their first jobs was to look over the whole Bahá'í world and formulate a teaching plan for the next five years that they could submit to the Universal House Justice. The Hands of the Cause and the Counsellors who were serving, travelled all over the world as part of their service, so they had understood what was going on and what needed to be done.

In her role as a Hand of the Cause at the International Teaching Centre, she travelled the entire world teaching and inspiring. Here is her itinerary for the last active decades of her life:

1977

- Return to India and Nepal: lay cornerstone of the Mother Temple of India in New Delhi, India
- Australia

1978

- Starting in June until February of next year—European countries; visit 35 centres in Japan and all four of its islands; Taiwan; Hong Kong; Macau; Samoa to lay cornerstone for the House of Worship, the Mother Temple of the Pacific; Fiji; New Hebrides; New Caledonia; New Zealand

1979

- June, Spain to dedicate of the Bahá'í Centre of Barcelona; Toronto, Canada, to edit 'The Pilgrimage' a documentary about the Bahá'í Holy Places
- August, Canada: conference for Auxiliary Board members at which they honoured the Hands who had passed
- December-January 1979 LA, and Vancouver to speak to large groups of Iranian and American Bahá'ís; Panama for the conference of Counsellors

1980

- January-July, Panama, Costa Rica, Nicaragua, Honduras, Belize, El Salvador, Guatemala, Mexico, the Bahamas, Bermuda, Antigua, Puerto Rico, the Dominican Republic, Haiti, Leeward Islands and Jamaica to talk about Faith to country leaders, encourage pioneers, meet Indigenous people, sometimes on foot
- August: Youth Conference in Kansas City, USA; UK: Scotland; and the northern islands—Shetland, Orkneys, Hebrides islands
- September: Cyprus, Greek and Turkish sections.

1982

- Dedication of the seat of the Universal House of Justice
- August: Conference on teaching Indigenous people
- October: Canada to visit Indigenous peoples in 45 locations: Magdalen Islands, Quebec, Cape Breton Island, Nova Scotia, Yukon Island, Newfoundland, Baffin Island, and Labrador, and Greenland (Denmark), and the country of Iceland.
- October-November: Haiti, travel length and breadth of the island, visit 25 communities, open the island of Isle a la Vache to the Faith.

1983

- July-September: Austrian Bahá'í youth Summer School; Cyprus summer school; Italy summer school

1984

- April 1984: First Convention of the Bahá'ís of the Andaman and Nicobar Islands.
- May: Travel across Korea, 12 locations
- June: Marina Islands (Rota, Saipan, Guam, Yap, Truk, Ponape, Majuro),
- July: Tuvalu, Fiji, Kiribati, Solomon Islands—visit grave of Knight of Bahá'u'lláh Alvin Blum; Papua New Guinea travel by helicopter and 14-meter-long dugout canoe
- September-October: Tonga, Australia, India
- November: India Sikkim

1985

- January: Brazil, two international Bahá'í conferences including one on the Amazon celebrating the 10 years of the Green Light Expedition; Panama
- November: present *Promise of World Peace* to the United Nations Secretary-General

1986

- July: Canada mostly northern Indigenous people—Yukon Bahá'í Institute. Dedication local Bahá'í Centre Montreal, same street as her childhood home, now a shrine. Then to Pine Ridge reservation in South Dakota
- August: Canada, Association for Bahá'í Studies; Bahá'í summer school in Sicily

- December: Dedication of the Mother Temple of India, 8,000 people, people from all states of India and from all over the world

1987

- January: visit Bahá'ís all over Thailand
- June: Hungary. Representative of the Universal House of Justice to the International Society for General Systems Research gathering of systems scientists—mathematics, physics, engineering, economics, management, and the biological and social sciences.
- October: Canada
- November: one month in France, visit Bahá'ís everywhere in that country, the largest Bahá'í gathering there up to that time took place.

1988

- April: Germany for celebration of 'Abdu'l-Bahá's 75th visit; Austria for same celebration
- July: China, private visit major cities; Hong Kong; Macau, opening of new Bahá'í centre; Taiwan

1989

- April: Macau, first election of the Macau Local Spiritual Assembly
- May/June: China Mongolia, Macau, Hong Kong
- November: Rúhíyyih Khánum opening the local Bahá'í Centre in Sheung Simi, Hong Kong,
- July: 33 days in Philippines

- August: 5 weeks in Taiwan; drove all over island, visited Indigenous people of Taiwan coastal village area; two weeks in Hong Kong
- September: 3 weeks in China with Kevin Locke

1990

- February: Argentina, 50th anniversary passing of mother, visits Indigenous area
- August-September: Spain for women's conference; Corsica
- September-October: Sakhalin Island; Tibet; China; Hainan island end to end

1991

- April: Romania, representative of Universal House Justice National Convention in Romania
- December: Canada for opening of exhibition on architecture of her father and brother; Bermuda

1992

- January: Canada
- April: representative of the Universal House of Justice at the National Convention of the Bahá'ís of Poland; Bulgaria, representative of the Universal House of Justice at the first National Convention of the Bahá'ís of Bulgaria
- November: Second Bahá'í World Congress

Rúhíyyih Khánum lived long enough to see the Second Bahá'í World Congress in New York City where she could see clear evidence by the wide variety of people in attendance, how much the Faith had grown all around the world.

One of the last public acts in the long and storied life of Rúhíyyih Khánum was to lay a scroll with the names of all the Knights of Bahá'u'lláh written on it beneath the entrance to the Shrine of Bahá'u'lláh. These were the individuals who had carried the Faith of Bahá'u'lláh around the world during the Ten-Year Crusade. Rúhíyyih Khánum spent decades after the passing of the Guardian doing the same—travelling over the entire planet to teach the Faith, encouraging Bahá'í pioneers, and remembering her husband with great love and telling of his great wisdom, humility, and greatness of vision.

She lived a unique life, one she could never ever have predicted or even planned. To live such a life requires faith. That is, complete trust or confidence. In what did Rúhíyyih Khánum have complete trust and confidence? In the existence of God and the Truth of the Manifestation of God, Bahá'u'lláh. As she was certain of this, she lived her life according to the teachings of the Faith. The decisions in her life were taken in the context of unshakable faith that she was walking the true path.

She wrote a poem about faith:

To walk where there is no path
To breathe where there is no air
To see where there is no light -
This is Faith.
To cry out in the silence,
The silence of the night,
And hearing no echo believe
And believe again and again -
This is Faith.
To hold pebbles and see jewels
To raise sticks and see forests
To smile with weeping eyes -
This is Faith.
To say: 'God, I believe' when others deny,
'I hear' when there is no answer,
'I see' though naught is seen -
This is Faith.

And the fierce love in the heart,
The savage love that cries
Hidden Thou art yet there!
Veil Thy face and mute Thy tongue
Yet I see and hear Thee, Love,
Beat me down to the bare earth,
Yet I rise and love Thee, Love!
This is Faith. [129]

Rúhíyyih Khánum passed away quietly in the house of ʻAbdu'l-Bahá on 19 January 2000, the Bahá'í year 176 B.E.

Rúhíyyih-Khannum with New York City Bahá'í Community.
Featuring Dr Peter Khan and author Hussein Ahdieh, 1976.

Rúhíyyih-Khannum and Violette Nakhjavani welcomed at
Kimpo airport, Korea, 1984.

Rúhíyyih Khánum greeted by His Highness Susuga Malietoa Tanumafili II,
and his wife, Masiofo Lili Tuni Malietoa. Samoa, 1984.

Rúhíyyih Khánum sweeping the deck.
Green Light Expedition, South America, 1975–76.

Rúhíyyih Khánum, circa 1970s.

Resting place of Rúhíyyih Khánum

On the Sunday afternoon that her precious remains were laid to rest, the sweetness of a chanted Persian prayer reverberated throughout the garden where nearly a thousand friends had gathered from places far-flung across the globe to pay tribute and homage to this beloved personage. A soft rain began to fall gently upon all there; perhaps nature's own testimony to the grief felt in all the hearts and the tears upon many a cheek.

Endnotes

[1]   Universal House of Justice, *Youth Conferences Announced by Universal House of Justice*, 8 February 1983.

[2]   'Abdu'l-Bahá, quoted in Violette Nakhjavani, "A Tribute to Amatu'l-Bahá Rúḥíyyih Khánum", https://www.bahai.org/documents/essays/nakhjavani-bahiyyih/tribute-amatulbaha-Rúḥíyyih-Khánum.

[3]   Nakhjavani, *The Maxwells, Vol. 1*, p. 11.

[4]   Ibid, p. 10.

[5]   Ibid, p. 53.

[6]   Lua Getsinger, Ibid, p. 70.

[7]   Agnes Alexander, Ibid, p. 71.

[8]   May Maxwell, Ibid, pp. 79-80.

[9]   May Maxwell, pilgrim's notes, 'Abdu'l-Bahá, Ibid, p. 74.

[10] May Maxwell, pilgrims notes, 'Abdu'l-Bahá, Ibid, p. 80.

[11] Henry Yates, Ibid, p. 57.

[12] May Maxwell, Ibid, p. 61.

[13] Ibid, p. 98.

[14] Sutherland Maxwell, Ibid, p. 110.

[15] May Bolles, Ibid, p. 114.

[16] 'Abdu'l-Bahá, Ibid, p. 181.

[17] May Maxwell, Ibid, p. 213.

[18] Conversation between Sutherland and May Maxwell and remembered by Rúḥíyyih Khánum, Ibid, p. 228.

[19] 'Abdu'l-Bahá, Ibid, p. 229.

[20] Ibid, p. 234.

[21] May Maxwell, Ibid, p. 234.

[22] Ibid, p. 251.

[23] 'Abdu'l-Bahá, Ibid, p. 268.

[24] Ibid, p. 275.

[25] Bahá'u'lláh, *The Tablet of the Branch*, quoted in Shoghi Effendi, *World Order of Bahá'u'lláh*, www.bahai.org/r/434537677

[26] Dodge, "'Abdu'l-Bahá's Arrival," *Star of the West*, 4.

[27] Shoghi Effendi, *God Passes By*, www.bahai.org/r/705725506

[28] Ibid.

[29] May Maxwell, quoted in Nakhjavani, *The Maxwells, Vol. 1*, p. 280.

[30]   'Abdu'l-Bahá, Ibid, p. 280.

[31]   Jack McLean, "Abdu'l-Bahá in Montreal,"
        https://bahai-library.com/mclean_centenary_abdulbaha_montreal

[32]   'Abdu'l-Bahá, *The Promulgation of Universal Peace*, p. 297.

[33]   Ibid, p. 312.

[34]   Rúhíyyih Khánum, quoted in Nakhjavani, *The Maxwells, Vol. 1*, p. 282.

[35]   Cable from 'Abdu'l-Bahá to May Maxwell, Ibid, p. 285.

[36]   May Maxwell, Ibid, pp. 314-315.

[37]   Mary Maxwell, Ibid, p. 317.

[38]   Ibid.

[39]   May Maxwell, Ibid, p. 342.

[40]   May Maxwell, Ibid, pp. 342-345.

[41]   Rabbani, *The Priceless Pearl*, p. 39.

[42]   Shoghi Effendi, quoted in Nakhjavani, *The Maxwells, Vol. 2*, p. 8.

[43]   Pilgrim's notes of May Maxwell, Ibid, p. 8.

[44]   Mary Maxwell, Ibid, p. 10.

[45]   Ibid, p. 15.

[46]   Ibid, p. 16.

[47]   May Maxwell, Ibid, p. 33.

[48]   May Maxwell, Ibid, p. 97.

[49]   Mary Maxwell, Ibid, p. 34.

[50]   May Maxwell, Ibid, p. 35.

[51]   Mary Maxwell, Ibid, p. 142.

[52]   Sutherland Maxwell, Ibid, p. 36.

[53]   Mary Maxwell, Ibid, pp. 64-65.

[54]   Mary Maxwell, pilgrims' notes, Ibid, p. 69.

[55]   Shoghi Effendi, Ibid, p. 69.

[56]   May Maxwell, Ibid, p. 69.

[57]   May Maxwell, Ibid, p. 190.

[58]   Mary Maxwell, Ibid, p. 214.

[59]   Shoghi Effendi, Ibid, p. 216.

[60]   Mary Maxwell, Ibid, p. 219,

[61]   May Maxwell, Ibid, p. 260.

[62]   Mary Maxwell, Ibid, p. 263.

[63]   Mary Maxwell, Ibid, p. 265.

[64] 'Abdu'l-Bahá, quoted in Rabbani, *The Priceless Pearl*, p. 1.

[65] Ibid, p. 2.

[66] Ella Cooper, Ibid, pp. 5-6.

[67] 'Abdu'l-Bahá, Ibid, p. 7.

[68] The Greatest Holy Leaf, Ibid, p. 7.

[69] 'Abdu'l-Bahá, Ibid, p. 9.

[70] Ibid.

[71] Ibid, p. 10.

[72] 'Abdu'l-Bahá, *The Will and Testament of 'Abdu'l-Bahá*, www.bahai.org/r/649191323

[73] Rúhíyyih Rabbani, Rabbani, *The Priceless Pearl*, p. 124.

[74] Ibid, p. 122.

[75] Ibid, p. 149.

[76] Ibid, p. 144.

[77] Response of Shoghi Effendi to a Spiritual Assembly in North America, Ibid, p. 153.

[78] Rúhíyyih Khánum, Ibid, pp. 162-3.

[79] Rúhíyyih Khánum, Ibid, p. 163.

[80] Rúhíyyih Khánum, Ibid, p. 160.

[81] Rúhíyyih Khánum, Ibid, p. 160.

[82] Ibid, p. 179.

[83] Rúhíyyih Khánum, Ibid, p. 162.

[84] Rúhíyyih Khánum, Ibid, p. 168.

[85] Rúhíyyih Khánum, Ibid, p. 168.

[86] Rúhíyyih Khánum, Ibid, p. 168.

[87] Ibid, p. 187.

[88] Shoghi Effendi, *The World Order of Bahá'u'lláh*, www.bahai.org/r/609410782

[89] Rúhíyyih Rabbani, Rabbani, *The Priceless Pearl*, p. 213.

[90] Ibid, p. 163.

[91] Shoghi Effendi in a letter to Martha Root, 3 March 1931, Ibid, p. 217.

[92] Ibid, p. 223.

[93] Ibid, p. 225.

[94] Ibid, p. 223.

[95] Shoghi Effendi, *Messages to the Bahá'í World: 1950-1957*.

[96] Ibid, pp. 152–153.

[97] Rúhíyyih Khánum, Rabbani, *The Priceless Pearl*, p. 410-411.

[98] Cable from Rúhíyyih Khánum to National Assemblies, November 5th, 1943, Ibid, p. 447.

[99] Rúhíyyih Khánum with John Ferraby, "The Passing of the Guardian," https://www.bahai.org/documents/essays/Rúhíyyih-Khánum-ferraby-john/passing-shoghi-effendi

[100] Rabbani, *Poems of the Passing*.

[101] "Proclamation by the Hands of the Cause to the Bahá'ís' of East and West," *Bahá'í World*, Vol. XIII, p. 341.

[102] Ibid, p. 342.

[103] Message from the Hands of the Cause in the Holy Land to the Intercontinental Conference in Kampala, Uganda, January 1958, https://bahai-library.com/uhj_ministry_custodians&chapter=2#56

[104] "Tribute to Shoghi Effendi by Rúhíyyih Khánum," 4, https://bahai.works/Bahá'í_News/Issue_327/Text

[105] Ibid, 4.

[106] Bahá'u'lláh, "Words of Paradise," www.bahai.org/r/723031566

[107] 'Abdu'l-Bahá, *Selections from the Writings of 'Abdu'l-Bahá*, www.bahai.org/r/139368998

[108] Shoghi Effendi, *The Advent of Divine Justice*, www.bahai.org/r/011656339

[109] Paul Haney, quoted in Linfoot, "First International Convention," *Bahá'í World* Vol. XIV, p. 429.

[110] Beatrice Ashton, "The Most Great Jubilee," *The Bahá'í World* 1963–1968, Vol. XIV, p. 62.

[111] Rúhíyyih Khánum, Ibid.

[112] Rúhíyyih Khánum, quoted in Nakhjavani, *Amatu'l-Bahá Visits India*, p. xix.

[113] Rúhíyyih Khánum, Ibid, pp. 18-19.

[114] Rúhíyyih Khánum, Ibid, p.49.

[115] Rúhíyyih Khánum, Ibid, pp. 64-65.

[116] Nakhjavani, Ibid, p. 95.

[117] Nakhjavani, Ibid, pp. 121-122.

[118] Rúhíyyih Khánum, Ibid, pp. 123-124.

[119] Rúhíyyih Khánum, quoted in Nakhjavani, "The Great Safari of Hand of the Cause Rúhíyyih Khánum," published in Bahá'í News #483, July 1971, pp. 16-20.

[120] Rúhíyyih Khánum, Ibid, #484, July 1971, pp. 17-20.

[121] Rúhíyyih Khánum, Ibid, #486, September 1971, pp. 18-22.

[122] Rúhíyyih Khánum, Ibid.

[123] Rúhíyyih Khánum, Ibid, #505, April 1973, pp. 16-20.

[124] Rúhíyyih Khánum, Ibid, #507, June 1973, pp. 18-21.

[125] Ibid.

[126] Rúhíyyih Khánum, Ibid, #513, December 1973, pp. 17-21.

[127] Rúhíyyih Khánum, quoted in Handal, *The Khamsis: A Cradle of Pure Faith*, pp. 255-269.

[128] 'Abdu'l-Bahá, *Tablets of the Divine Plan*, www.bahai.org/r/254714407

[129] Rúhíyyih Khánum, *This is Faith*.

Bibliography

Bahá'u'lláh

"Words of Paradise,"
  https://bahai.works/Tablets_of_Bahá'u'lláh/Words_of_Paradise

'Abdu'l-Bahá

Selections from the Writings of 'Abdu'l-Bahá,
  https://www.bahai.org/library/authoritative-texts/abdul-baha/selections-writings-abdul-baha/

Tablets of the Divine Plan,
  https://www.bahai.org/library/authoritative-texts/abdul-baha/tablets-divine-plan/

The Will and Testament of 'Abdu'l-Bahá,
  https://www.bahai.org/library/authoritative-texts/abdul-baha/will-testament-abdul-baha/

Shoghi Effendi

World Order of Bahá'u'lláh,
  https://www.bahai.org/library/authoritative-texts/shoghi-effendi/world-order-bahaullah/

God Passes By,
  https://www.bahai.org/library/authoritative-texts/shoghi-effendi/god-passes-by/

Messages to the Bahá'í World. Bahá'í Publishing Trust: Wilmette IL. 1971.

The Advent of Divine Justice,
  https://www.bahai.org/library/authoritative-texts/shoghi-effendi/advent-divine-justice/

Universal House of Justice

Youth Conferences Announced by Universal House of Justice, 8 February 1983.

Authors

Beatrice Ashton. "The Most Great Jubilee." *The Bahá'í World 1963-1968, Vol. XIV.*
https://bahai.works/Bahái_World/Volume_14

Arthur P. Dodge. "'Abdu'l-Bahá's Arrival." *Star of the West, v. 3, #3.*
https://bahai.works/Star_of_the_West/Volume_3/Issue_3/Text.

Boris Handal. *The Khamsis: A Cradle of Pure Faith.* Self-Published, Boris Handal. 2020.

Charlotte Linfoot. "First International Convention." *Bahá'í World Vol. XIV*
https://bahai.works/Bahái_World/Volume_14

Jack McLean. "Abdu'l-Baha in Montreal."
https://bahai-library.com/mclean_centenary_abdulbaha_montreal

Message from the Hands of the Cause in the Holy Land to the Intercontinental Conference in Kampala, Uganda, January 1958.
https://bahai-library.com/uhj_ministry_custodians&chapter=2#56

"Proclamation by the Hands of the Cause to the Bahá'ís of East and West," Bahá'í World, XIII, 341
https://bahai.works/Bahái_World/Volume_13

Violette Nakhjavani, with Bahiyyih Nakhjavani. *The Maxwells of Montreal: Vol. 1.* George Ronald Publisher: Oxford, UK. 2011.

Violette Nakhjavani, with Bahiyyih Nakhjavani. *The Maxwells of Montreal: Vol. 2.* George Ronald Publisher: Oxford, UK. 2012.

Violette Nakhjavani. *Amatu'l-Bahá Visits India.* Bahá'í Publishing Trust: New Delhi, India. 1966.

Violette Nakhjavani. "A Tribute to Amatu'l-Bahá Rúhíyyih Khánum."
https://www.bahai.org/documents/essays/nakhjavani-bahiyyih/tribute-amatulbaha-Rúhíyyih-Khánum

Violette Nakhjavani, *The Great Safari of Hand of the Cause Rúhíyyih Khánum.* Serialised in *Bahá'í News, 1970-3* and later published as *The Great African Safari – The travels of Rúhíyyih Khánum in Africa, 1969-73*, by George Ronald Publisher. 2000.

Rúhíyyih Rabbani. *The Priceless Pearl.* Bahá'í Publishing: London, UK. 1969.

Rúhíyyih Rabbani. *Poems of the Passing.* George Ronald Publisher: Oxford, UK. 1996.

Rúhíyyih Rabbani. *This is Faith.*
https://bahai-library.com/Khánum_this_is_faith

Rúhíyyih Khánum with John Ferraby. "The Passing of the Guardian."
https://www.bahai.org/documents/essays/Rúhíyyih-Khánum-ferraby-john/passing-shoghi-effendi

Yas. "Amatu'l-Baha Rúhíyyih Khánum."
https://www.bahaiblog.net/articles/history-tributes/amatul-baha-Rúhíyyih-Khánum-mary-sutherland-maxwell/

Image Bibliography

p. 23. May and Mary Maxwel, circa late 1910.
Courtesy of Baháí Media website, contributed by "Mrjames"
https://bahai.media/File:Famatp~03m~amat-portrait.jpg

p. 24. May and Mary Maxwel, circa late 1910.
Courtesy of Baháí Stories website, author Farhad Naderi
http://bahaistories.blogspot.com/2015/03/the-story-of-how-abdul-baha-blessed-may.html

p. 25. Mary Maxwel, circa 1914.
Copyright © Baháí International Community
https://media.bahai.org/detail/2011283/

p. 26. May and Mary Maxwell in Alexandria, Egypt, 1923.
Copyright © Baháí International Community
http://media.bahai.org/subjects/6460/details

p. 27. Mary Waxwell, circa 1926.
Courtesy of Baháí Media website, contributed by "Mrjames"
https://bahai.media/File:Rúhíyyih_Khánum_Aged_16.jpg

p. 28. Mary Waxwell, circa 1926.
Courtesy of Baháí Chronicles website, photo by John Yazdi
https://bahaichronicles.org/amatul-baha-Rúhíyyih-Khánum/

p. 29. Mary Waxwell, summer 1934.
Copyright © Baháí International Community
https://bahai.media/File:Maxwell_William-and-Mary_1948.jpg

p. 30. William Sutherland Waxwell.
Copyright © Baháí International Community
https://media.bahai.org/detail/1552588/

p. 159. Shoghi Effendi, 1919.
Copyright © Baháí International Community
https://media.bahai.org/detail/fd8dddd8dce42614549297d9d7382ee2/

p. 268. Rúhíyyih Khánum greeted by His Highness Susuga Malietoa Tanumafili II, and his wife, Masiofo Lili Tuni Malietoa. Samoa, 1984.
Copyright © Baháʼí International Community
https://media.bahai.org/detail/2560712/

p. 268. Rúhíyyih Khánum sweeping the deck. South America, 1975-76.
Copyright ©National Spiritual Assembly of the Baháʼís of the United States
https://file.bahai.media/c/cd/Slide_054_-_Rúhíyyih_Rabbani_sweeping_the_deck_of_the_ship.png

p. 269. Rúhíyyih Khánum, circa 1970s.
Copyright © Baháʼí International Community
https://media.bahai.org/detail/1586815/

p. 270. Resting place of Rúhíyyih Khánum.
Copyright © Baháʼí International Community
https://media.bahai.org/detail/2453064/

Made in the USA
Las Vegas, NV
30 May 2025

7358f4bd-5535-4a18-ae90-7b4bf93a9eebR01